MW00852152

"Bruce Tremper has dor
able and usable framew
His stories and dramatic photos underline his message."

AVALANCHE
ESSENTIALS

AVALANCHE ESSENTIALS

A STEP-BY-STEP
SYSTEM FOR SAFETY
AND SURVIVAL

Bruce Tremper

MOUNTAINEERS
BOOKS

DEDICATION

To my wife, Susi—my soul mate, best friend,
best outdoor adventuring partner, and love of my life

Mountaineers Books is the nonprofit publishing division of The Mountaineers, an organization founded in 1906 and dedicated to the exploration, preservation, and enjoyment of outdoor and wilderness areas.

MOUNTAINEERS
BOOKS

1001 SW Klickitat Way, Suite 201 • Seattle, WA 98134
800.553.4453 • www.mountaineersbooks.org

First edition: first printing 2013, second printing 2015, third printing 2018

Distributed in the United Kingdom by Cordee, www.cordee.co.uk

Manufactured in the United States of America

Copy editor: Erin Moore
Cover, design and layout: Peggy Egerdahl
Illustrator: Gray Mouse Graphics
All photographs by author unless otherwise noted.

Cover photograph: *Caroline Gleich, Kessler Peak, Wasatch Range, Utah*
    © Jay Beyer Imaging

Library of Congress Cataloging-in-Publication Data
Tremper, Bruce, 1953-
 Avalanche essentials : a step-by-step system for safety and survival / Bruce Tremper.
   pages cm
 Includes index.
 ISBN 978-1-59485-717-1 (ppb)
1. Mountaineering—Safety measures. 2. Avalanches—Accidents. 3. Avalanches—Safety measures. 4. Skis and skiing—Safety measures. I. Title.
 GV200.18.T73 2013
 796.522—dc23

ISBN (paperback): 978-1-59485-717-1
ISBN (ebook): 978-1-59485-718-8

CONTENTS

ACKNOWLEDGMENTS

I especially want to thank my friends who reviewed the sections of the manuscript in their area of expertise, found my many errors, and offered valuable suggestions. In alphabetical order:

Dale Atkins (president, American Avalanche Association)

Tyson Bradley (Utah Mountain Adventures)

Brian Lazar (Colorado Avalanche Information Center and AIARE)

Ian McCammon (avalanche educator; now working in risk management)

Wendy Wagner (Chugach Avalanche Center)

Lynn Wolfe (editor, *The Avalanche Review*)

Thanks to the many people who contributed graphics, data, research, and long brainstorming sessions. At the Swiss Federal Institute of Snow and Avalanche Research: Stephen Harvey, Manuel Genswein, Jürg Schweizer, Chris Pielmeier, and Werner Munter; my New Zealand friends Andrew (Hobbie) Hobman and Gordon Smith; the amazing Karl Birkeland, director of the Forest Service National Avalanche Center; all my Canadian friends, especially Pascal Haegeli, Grant Statham, Karl Klassen, and Roger Atkins; and, of course, my longtime Alaska friends and mentors, Jill Fredston and Doug Fesler.

Thanks to my editors and project managers at Mountaineers Books: Kate Rogers, Margaret Sullivan, Kris Fulsaas, Janet Kimball, and especially Erin Moore.

Finally, a special thanks to my long-suffering wife, Susi, who put up with the seemingly endless days of work, all done after hours from my regular job, plus many weekends and holidays.

INTRODUCTION:
WHY SHOULD YOU CARE?

I was astoundingly lucky to be born into a mountain culture and learn about mountains and avalanches from the top professionals in the country. When I was ten years old, my father, a volunteer ski patroller, took an avalanche class from Dr. John Montagne, who taught the first university avalanche class in the country at Montana State University in Bozeman. I remember he came home excited after a multiday course and tried to teach me what he learned. (And I also remember being not a particularly good student at the age of ten.)

Fifteen years later, after a successful ski-racing career, I landed a job doing avalanche control on the Bridger Bowl Ski Patrol in Bozeman, where I was trained by some of the best, most experienced avalanche professionals in the country. I took the quarter-long course from my father's avalanche instructor, Dr. Montagne, who later became my thesis advisor for an avalanche-related study for my master's in geology.

I've worked doing mountain rescues in both Grand Teton National Park and Glacier National Park, served as director of avalanche control at Big Sky Ski Area in Montana, and worked with avalanche forecasters Jill Fredston and Doug Fesler at the Alaska Avalanche Center. And finally, for nearly three decades, I've been the director of the Utah Avalanche Center, where you can't throw a snowball without hitting an avalanche expert.

I was trained in the *system*. In the *system*, everyone practices rigorous procedures and decision making, low-risk travel rituals, and disciplined communication learned by trial and error over many years by avalanche professionals.

The backcountry, on the other hand, is chaos. I see hundreds of people racing for powder, on skis, snowmobiles, snowboards, and snowshoes, and on foot. Some have avalanche rescue gear; some do not.

I see people routinely violate all the standard practices I was taught as a professional: People bunched up and talking instead of being spread out and paying attention; people traveling above other parties—considered attempted homicide in professional operations. I see people jump into zero-tolerance-for-error terrain, where an avalanche of any size would be certain death, when they could have easily chosen a gentler spur ridge off to the side with much safer consequences. I see people dive into huge, steep bowls on the first run instead of doing a few stability tests on smaller test slopes first. I seldom see people test their beacons before leaving the parking lot (required each morning by pros) or practice rescue techniques (required once per month by pros). And so on.

As a result, an average of 30 people die in avalanches each season in the United States and 15 per season in Canada, yet only 1.4 percent of these accidents occur to professional avalanche workers despite far greater exposure. Why is that?

This book on avalanche essentials presents a step-by-step system for safety and survival that I learned from 35 years as an avalanche professional. It presents systematic ways to make evidence-based decisions to travel safely in backcountry avalanche terrain, and explains what to do when things go wrong.

A TALE OF TWO ACCIDENTS

Below is a comparison of two actual avalanche accidents. In both cases, someone made a mistake. So why did one accident end in tragedy while the other did not? Can you spot what caused the difference in outcome?

Avalanche Accident #1

The day after Christmas I got a call that the Salt Lake County Search and Rescue was looking for an overdue snowboarder. The previous day he had failed to pick up his girlfriend from the airport, and that night the sheriff discovered his vehicle parked on the road near Alta Ski Area. His roommates reported that he went up to take a quick backcountry run on his snowboard before he went to the airport on what happened to be the first day of a major winter storm.

That day our avalanche advisory had warned the public of rapidly increasing avalanche danger, especially on the northerly facing slopes. Based on the location of his vehicle and recent avalanche activity, we speculated that he had booted up the popular south-facing Flagstaff Ridge to take a run in the fresh powder on the north side of the ridge and must have triggered an avalanche there. The only encouraging news was that he almost always wore his avalanche rescue beacon so at least he would be easy to locate.

I teamed up with my good friend Al Soucie, the Forest Service snow ranger at Alta, who used to work for me as an avalanche forecaster at the Utah Avalanche Center. As the storm was ending, we broke a trail up the safe, wind-scoured, south-facing Flagstaff Ridge, and we spent the rest of the day searching for the snowboarder's beacon signal on the north side of the ridge under countless acres of fresh avalanche debris in several different slide paths. But we found no beacon signal and returned home tired and discouraged.

The next day, I teamed up with another good friend, Dave Medara, an avalanche forecaster for the Utah Department of Transportation. Since Al and I had not found the snowboarder on the north side of the ridge, we thought that perhaps he had triggered an avalanche on the south side above the highway, although we had not noticed any slides there during the previous day's search.

Sure enough, we found one small avalanche that, in the poor visibility, we had not seen before. We found the snowboarder's beacon signal and extricated his body under about 2 feet of debris. Apparently, he had been boarding alone and triggered

Photo I-1. This is a popular backcountry area next to a busy road, but if you put your avalanche eyeballs on, you can see it also contains a nasty terrain trap. The terrain funnels into a narrow gully where even a small avalanche could bury you deeply, first straining you through trees on the way down. The standard ascent route is along the left skyline ridge, which is much safer than the terrain trap in the middle of the photo. This is where we found the snowboarder in Avalanche Accident #1, and it has been the site of many close calls, too.

a slab avalanche composed of wind-drifted snow high on the shoulder of the ridge, which then funneled down into a narrow gully far below (see Photo I-1). Because of the funnel shape, which terminates in a narrow gully we call a "terrain trap," even a small avalanche can bury a victim deeply.

The snowboarder was a handsome young man who seemed like someone I would have liked. Later, in the command center, as I explained to his friends and girlfriend how we had found him and what must have happened, I gave them my condolences through teary eyes all around, including mine.

Avalanche Accident #2

Coincidentally, this second accident, in a different year, involved the same two people, Al Soucie and Dave Medara, who had searched with me in the accident just described. Just as coincidentally, this accident also occurred on a slope near where Accident #1 took place.

As part of their job, Al and Dave had broken a trail up Flagstaff Ridge to do snow profile tests on the south-facing slopes that threaten the highway below. When they neared the bottom of the ridge they decided to descend a gentle avalanche bed surface where a recent avalanche had occurred, which is almost always a very safe procedure. Al descended to the bottom of the short slope and waited at the far edge of the debris pile. As Dave descended, he triggered a deep slab avalanche about 3 feet (1 meter) deep on the bed surface of the previous slide, an extremely rare occurrence. Since it was such a gentle slope and the slab moved slowly, Dave was able to scramble off the moving slab, but the unexpectedly large avalanche overran Al's location and buried him.

Dave immediately descended on the bed surface and quickly located Al with his avalanche rescue beacon. Dave dug him out in time to save his life.

What Was the Difference?

The difference in outcome between these two accidents in nearly the same location is due to the second party using what I call a "system." Avalanche professionals ritualistically operate in a time-tested system of procedures and safety nets, which include:

- ❖ training
- ❖ mentoring
- ❖ decision-making procedures
- ❖ safety equipment
- ❖ low-risk travel practices
- ❖ communication
- ❖ rescue

Al and Dave are avalanche pros, and they always operate within this safety system. Both were trained and mentored in the crucible of some of the best avalanche professionals in the country right there in Little Cottonwood Canyon. Both were taught on their first day of work that they *always* traveled with a skilled partner, *always* wore an avalanche beacon, and *always* carried a shovel and probe in their pack. They always spread out when they traveled and always exposed only one person at a time to the hazard while the other person always waited in a safe spot to do the rescue in case something went wrong. They always made their snow stability and routefinding decisions in a systematic way. They always communicated with each other in a systematic way, and they always did avalanche rescue practice a minimum of once per month. No exceptions.

This system attempts to minimize decision-making errors, but it also assumes that even the best people are fallible and unforeseen events will occur. In these cases the system helps to minimize the damage from our inevitable mistakes, so we can survive the experience. This book is intended to help you be one of the survivors.

Vision Zero

Avalanche professionals are not the only ones to use this kind of system. Similar time-tested procedures, checklists, and rules are widely used by people working in commercial aviation, the stock market, the medical field, military, industry, and many other environments where mistakes could be fatal.

A program in Sweden called "Vision Zero" is an example. It was adopted in 1997 as an attempt to reduce automobile accident fatalities to zero. This bold initiative presented a complete paradigm shift in risk management thinking.

Traditional approaches to car-accident reduction relied heavily on car drivers taking personal responsibility to make safe decisions. Vision Zero, on the other hand, focused on shared responsibility. Rather than try the impossible task of perfecting human behavior, Vision Zero accommodates human failings in its design. The entire Swedish highway system is designed to keep accidents to a minimum but also to allow drivers to survive inevitable mistakes and unforeseen events. This is accomplished through better engineering of roads and cars to favor safety as much as or more than mobility. Vision Zero also uses education, peer pressure, and more of a market-based than a regulatory approach.

Because of Vision Zero, the fatality rate in automobile crashes per capita in Sweden decreased much faster than in the United States. In 1970, the fatality rate in Sweden was higher than in the United States; it now has a fatality rate only one quarter of the United States'. Today, Vision Zero has been adopted by many states in the United States.

POPULAR MYTHS ABOUT AVALANCHES
(AND WHAT REALLY CAUSES AVALANCHE FATALITIES)

MYTH "Noise triggers avalanches."

TRUTH Only in the movies. In 35 years as an avalanche professional I have never once seen an avalanche triggered by, say, a shout or even a sonic boom. I have heard of very rare incidents where low-flying helicopters triggered avalanches in extremely unstable conditions—most likely because of rotor wash, however, not noise. Most noise just does not exert enough force. Even with an explosive charge, it's not the noise but the shock wave that is the trigger. In 93 percent of US avalanche fatalities, the avalanche was triggered by the weight of the victim or someone in the victim's party.

MYTH "An avalanche is a bunch of loose snow sliding down the mountain."

TRUTH Technically, yes, but avalanche professionals call these "sluffs," or loose snow avalanches, which account for only a small percentage of deaths and property damage. When we talk about avalanches, we generally mean "slab" avalanches—cohesive plates of snow sliding as a unit. Picture a magazine sliding off an inclined table, with the victim standing on the middle of the magazine.

MYTH "Avalanches strike without warning."

TRUTH I often hear the word "strike" used in the popular media. Earthquakes, meteoroid impacts, love and lost love may strike without warning, but avalanches usually have obvious signs. In addition, avalanches don't "strike." They happen at particular times and in particular places for particular reasons. *In 93 percent of all avalanche accidents, the avalanche is triggered by the victim or someone in the victim's party.* Natural avalanches occur because new or windblown snow overloads weak layers or because of rapid warming or rain, but there are usually clear signs of instability by the time avalanches come down on their own.

POPULAR MYTHS ABOUT AVALANCHES
(AND WHAT REALLY CAUSES AVALANCHE FATALITIES)
(CONTINUED)

MYTH "If you see an avalanche coming, get out of the way."

TRUTH Good luck. An average-size dry avalanche travels 60 to 120 kilometers per hour (60 to 80 miles per hour), so you'll need to be mighty cagey and mighty quick to get out of the way. People have been known to scoot off to the side in time, especially on a snowmobile, but as far as outrunning an avalanche, you will need to be either a world-class athlete or a very good driver of a very fast snowmobile with no obstacles in the way. Also, naturally triggered avalanches that descend from above kill few people. Do I sound like a broken record here? The vast majority of avalanche incidents are triggered by the victim or someone in the victim's party.

MYTH "When buried in an avalanche, spit to tell which way is up and dig in that direction."

TRUTH It doesn't matter which way is up. You can't dig yourself out. If you could dig yourself out, few people would die in avalanches. Avalanche debris instantly entombs you in place, as if you were frozen in concrete, and most of the time you can't even move your fingers. Sometimes, if it's a small avalanche with soft debris and they have a hand near the surface, people have been able to dig themselves out. For almost all completely buried victims, there are only two ways to get out of the snow—to be dug out or to melt out.

MYTH "All the avalanche experts are dead."

TRUTH Realizing that it may be bad luck to even say this, I'm happy to report that just the opposite is true. In the United States skilled avalanche professionals enjoy a very low avalanche fatality rate compared to other groups, especially when you consider the amount of time an avalanche professional spends in dangerous avalanche terrain. Only 1.4 percent of all avalanche fatalities involve avalanche professionals.

The Systems Approach

The individual may be fallible, but the system is wise. The system is a time-tested series of procedures and safety nets. For avalanche safety, that system includes these steps:

1. Make pretrip plans.
2. Gather information.
3. Know what kind of avalanches you are dealing with.
4. Know what the pattern is.
5. Choose terrain based on those patterns.
6. Know how to travel on the terrain.
7. Know what to do if things go wrong.

If our behavior, decision-making skills, and rescue skills are random or chaotic, then so might be our death. Our habits can either save our life or kill us. Thus, developing good habits through the same careful system developed by professionals gives us the best chance to avoid an untimely and tragic death in an avalanche.

A NOTE ABOUT MEASUREMENT UNITS

The United States is the only industrialized country that doesn't use the metric system, which certainly makes the avalanche business difficult. While scientists everywhere in the world use the metric system, the US National Weather Service still communicates to the public in US units. To make this book understandable to all readers and to conform to international standards, I use metric units followed by their US unit equivalents.

WHAT HAPPENS WHEN YOU GET CAUGHT IN AN AVALANCHE?

One out of four avalanche fatalities in the United States and Canada dies from trauma from hitting trees and rocks on the way down. Of those who survive the ride, the lucky ones end up with their head above the surface or close enough to the surface to breathe, and they or their partners can often dig them out. Completely buried victims begin a desperate race against time, in which less than half will live.

There is plenty of air in the snow that we can breathe. That's not the problem.

Avalanche victims die from re-breathing their own carbon dioxide (hypercapnia) rather than from a lack of oxygen. Moreover, the condensation of the victim's breath forms an "ice mask" around their mouth, further exacerbating the buildup of deadly carbon dioxide.

How much time do you have? Not long. As rescue times have become shorter in recent years, we have discovered that completely buried victims are dying faster

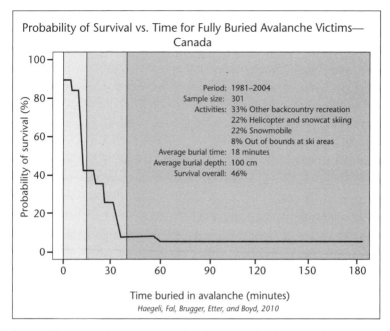

Figure I-1. The latest survival curve uses data from Canada, showing that completely buried avalanche victims do not last long under the snow. Less than half of those completely buried survive, and those who do live do so only through very fast rescue by companions. It is much better to avoid avalanche burial than to count on surviving one. Notice that about half of completely buried victims die in the first 15 minutes and 90 percent die in the first 40 minutes. But you can never give up hope because about 8 percent have some sort of air pocket and can be recovered alive for some time.

under the snow than we previously thought, as in Figure I-1's graph of Canadian avalanche victims. Although the US data has not been plotted in a similar way, the Canadian data probably matches our situation, because in the United States as in Canada many accidents occur near tree line where the incidence of trauma is higher. These dire survival curves match my experience investigating US avalanche accidents, mostly in Montana, Alaska, and Utah.

Avalanche victims are like drowning victims. They have to be dug out of the snow *fast*. If the victim is wearing an avalanche rescue beacon (see Chapter 8, Rescue Technology) *and* their partners escape or survive the slide *and* those partners have been regularly practicing with their beacons, then they have a chance to dig

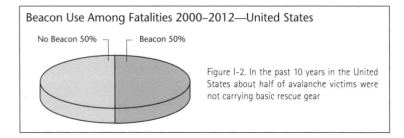

Beacon Use Among Fatalities 2000–2012—United States

No Beacon 50% —⌐   ⌐— Beacon 50%

Figure I-2. In the past 10 years in the United States about half of avalanche victims were not carrying basic rescue gear

the victim out in time—but this doesn't happen very often, as shown in Figure I-2. One half of those who die in avalanches are not wearing a beacon.

In practice, for approximately every 10 people who die in an avalanche, only 1 is rescued from a complete burial by their partners or other rescuers. The numbers usually don't add up to many happy endings.

If you have come to the conclusion that avalanches are dangerous and avalanche rescue does not work very well, then you have passed the test: Read on.

WHERE DO PEOPLE GET KILLED IN AVALANCHES?

Ski area personnel and highway transportation departments do an extremely thorough job of forecasting avalanches and controlling them with explosives before people arrive each morning. Because of this, since 1980, fewer than 1 percent of avalanche fatalities have occurred within ski area boundaries on open runs or on open highways. At least in the United States, you stand a much greater chance of being killed by lightning than by an inbounds or highway avalanche.

The vast majority of avalanche incidents occur in the backcountry, defined as areas outside of ski area boundaries where no systematic avalanche control is done. Although highway departments often conduct avalanche control with explosives to protect high-risk sections of the highway, those slopes are still considered backcountry because they only control for large avalanches that might hit the road and not for smaller avalanches that people might trigger. The same goes for terrain occasionally controlled with explosives by helicopter skiing companies.

TAKE-HOME POINT

Everyone who goes into uncontrolled backcountry avalanche terrain can be at risk: Everyone needs to have basic avalanche education, needs to carry avalanche rescue gear, and needs to check the avalanche advisory before heading out.

Photo I-2. Very subtle differences in steepness, aspect, and what the slope is connected to can make all the difference in the world. Four skiers descended on the gentler terrain, south facing, on the right of the photo. Then the last skier decided to descend terrain that was slightly closer to the much steeper, more easterly facing slope. He triggered the avalanche remotely, luckily noticed it, and jetted off to the side. In this case, the skier triggered a persistent weak layer, which was buried under the new snow on the more easterly facing slopes but not on the south-facing slopes where the first four skiers descended.

WHO GETS KILLED IN AVALANCHES?

When I first started my avalanche career 35 years ago, avalanche fatalities were not only relatively rare, they occurred mostly to backcountry skiers wearing wool knickers and skinny wooden skis and, to a few intrepid mountaineers on big mountains. Since then, avalanche demographics have been completely turned upside down. Today, skiers and climbers represent the minority compared to the new kids on the block: snowmobilers and, to a lesser extent, snowboarders. Among skiers, the trend is clearly toward more extreme athletes on heavier, wider equipment skiing closer to roads and ski area boundaries.

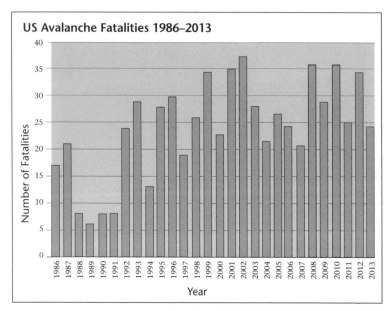

Figure I-3. About 30 people per year die in avalanches in the United States and 15 per year in Canada. Encouragingly, the trend in recent years has remained relatively flat.

TAKE-HOME POINT

Almost all avalanche fatalities involve recreationists, most notably snowmobilers, backcountry skiers, snowboarders, and climbers—in that order.

Fifteen years ago, existing technology did not allow snowmobilers to access the backcountry right after a storm. But led by hill-climbing pioneers who tinkered in their garages, equipment manufacturers now build high-performance mountain snowmobiles, which can now go virtually any place a skier can go and cover 10 to 100 times more terrain than a skier in a day and in nearly any kind of snow condition. So if there are any instabilities out there, a snowmobiler can easily find them. Nearly overnight, it seems, remote mountain ranges once accessible only to superfit skiers on multiday trips are now completely tracked by snowmobilers after a sunny powder weekend. Today, large new populations of people with little experience with snow, or knowledge or understanding of avalanches, have easy access to thousands of square miles of pristine avalanche terrain.

Similar but less dramatic accident spikes have occurred among a new generation of mountain aficionados, snowboarders, snowshoers, and skiers on superwide skis. Skis, snowboards, snowshoes, and climbing equipment have made quantum leaps in performance, weight, and variety. The sales of backcountry skiing and snowboarding equipment have rapidly increased while the sales of resort skiing and boarding equipment have remained flat or decreased. Ski resorts routinely market their adjacent, uncontrolled "sidecountry" but don't be fooled; sidecountry is really uncontrolled backcountry where you can quickly get into trouble without training and rescue gear. Several avalanche fatalities occur each year in the United States in out-of-bounds areas near ski resorts. Dozens of extreme video companies glorify big mountain riding and the thrill of the backcountry, yet few of them ever show basic safety procedures.

The profile of recreationists has changed dramatically in recent years. The high mountains used to be the exclusive playground of climbers and skiers, but they have since become the minority compared with rapidly increasing numbers of snowmobilers, snowboarders, snowshoers, hunters, hikers, and Boy Scout troops. This translates into more people in the mountains, going more places more often, so the flat trend in recent years is a good sign.

Whatever your sport—snowmobiling, skiing, snowboarding, climbing, or snowshoeing—it's hard to pick up a magazine or watch a video without succumbing to the siren call: images of elite, handsome athletes in stunning scenery, performing on the cutting edge of their sport, and almost always in very dangerous avalanche terrain.

Yet the visuals almost never show what goes on behind the scenes—the many days of research and preparation by their guides and safety crew to allow the athletes and film crew to operate safely. Nor do they show rehab from blown-out knees and broken bones, people in wheelchairs, the tears from loved ones at the many memorial services for mountain athletes that occur around the country every year.

Media reports often state that the victims were "experienced," meaning that they were skilled at their sport, yet they seldom mention that their avalanche skills lagged far behind their sport skills, which is almost invariably the case. Possibly because they are strong skiers, boarders, or snowmobilers, nearly all avalanche victims overestimate their avalanche skills—usually vastly overestimate them. Combine these facts with a dearth of funding for public avalanche information services and the fact that avalanche training videos, books, and classes are scarce and poorly funded, and it's easy to see why many encounters with avalanches end badly.

It seems to be a man-thing, like talking about grizzly bears or hunting or starting a fire in the woods. We puff up our chests, tell our lies, and would literally rather die than admit our ineptitude. There must be a reason, after all, why 92 percent of

Photo I-3. Forested glades feel safer than they really are. A friend of mine broke both his legs after his party triggered a large, deep slab avalanche on the steep, rocky slope. The slope had many previous ski tracks on it, which helped lure them into a false sense of security. The avalanche sent my friend into a tree at high speed. He was rescued barely in time to save his life.

avalanche fatalities are men and only 8 percent, women. (These numbers, perhaps not coincidentally, are similar percentages as males to females in the US prison population.)

Good News—Bad News

In the past, avalanche knowledge was the exclusive domain of skiers and climbers, but avalanche centers such as the one where I work in Utah have had to scramble to keep up with rapidly changing demographics. Avalanche professionals have struggled to spread avalanche classes and avalanche bulletins into new user groups that often have little contact with one another. We've also had to adapt that knowledge to a whole new culture and language, and to new equipment and travel styles. Partly because of these intensive efforts to bring snowmobilers into the avalanche community, there has been a very encouraging trend toward more education, greater use of rescue gear, and fewer fatalaties among snowmobilers.

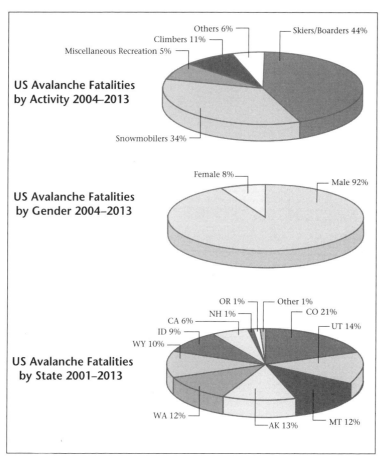

Figure I-4. US avalanche fatalities by activity, gender, and state. See Figure I-5 for fatalities by age and decade. CAIC National Database.

TAKE-HOME POINT

Almost all avalanche fatalities in recent decades have been males, very skilled in their sport, fit, educated, intelligent, middle class, and between the ages of 18 and 40 (Figures I-4 and I-5). Does this sound anything like you or someone you love?

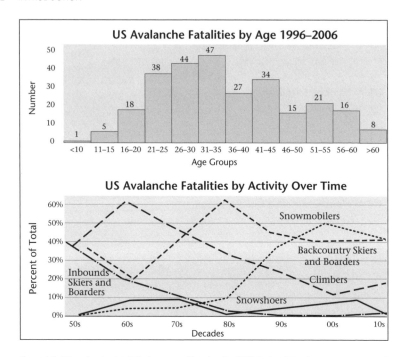

Figure I-5. US avalanche fatalities by age and by decade. CAIC National Database

Yet responsible recreation in backcountry avalanche terrain is probably not as dangerous as most people imagine. The daily risk of driving your car is probably equally or more dangerous than responsible backcountry recreation using all the risk reduction measures taught in avalanche classes. Contrarily, if you randomly jump into avalanche slopes at a considerable danger rating without using risk reduction measures, the risk is about the same as base jumping, which is one of the most dangerous sports in the world.

Yet, in many ways, avalanches are surprisingly benevolent. Only about 1 out of 10 people caught in an avalanche will die in an avalanche. So avalanches usually give us a number of cheap lessons before we get an expensive one. The trouble comes when we don't survive the lesson.

Finally, in 93 percent of avalanche accidents, the avalanche is triggered by the victim or someone in the victim's party.

This is good news because we have two important things going for use. First, we have the power to choose our own destiny in the backcountry: We can choose where and when to go, armed with knowledge about snow, terrain, and avalanches. Second, we already know the enemy. The bad news is that, as the Pogo cartoon says, "We have met the enemy and he is us"—and that is the hardest enemy of all to conquer.

LEARNING ABOUT AVALANCHES THE HARD WAY

Nearly every one of us has to learn about avalanches the hard way, and I'm certainly no exception. Short of getting killed, I must have made every mistake possible. I've taken a couple of very frightening rides in avalanches, and I've worn a brace on my knee for a month because of one of them. On several occasions, I've had to ski off of moving slabs I triggered. I've cried over the deaths of students, friends, and even a coworker, blaming myself for not teaching them enough.

I'm not sure what it is about avalanches and backcountry travel, but people invariably overestimate their skills.

I think one of the major contributing factors is known as "poor feedback environment." From my experience, any particular avalanche slope is stable 95 percent of the time; so even if you know absolutely nothing about avalanches, you automatically get a 19-out-of-20-times success rate. In other words, we get rewarded for bad behavior. You go out into avalanche terrain, nothing happens. You go out again, nothing happens. You go out again and again and again; still no avalanches. Yes, there's nothing like success! (See Chapter 1, How Dangerous Is the Brain?)

The frightening truth is that in most close calls, the average person has no idea they even had a close call because they didn't trigger an avalanche—kind of like playing soccer on a minefield. You didn't weigh *quite* enough to set the thing off.

In an ideal world, everyone would take a multiday avalanche class then buy a beacon, probe, and shovel and practice with them. Finally, when they felt ready, they would venture into lower-risk avalanche terrain, working their way into increasingly hazardous terrain as they gained confidence in their snow and avalanche skills.

What happens in the real world? Just the opposite. While we're still in the ignorance-is-bliss stage, we jump into one steep slope after another, coming home 95 percent of the time with smiles on our faces because, after all, in my experience snow is stable about 95 percent of the time.

But if a slope can produce an avalanche, it eventually will. When the inevitable happens, we get an expensive lesson, whereupon we realize that maybe we should buy one of those "beepers." After a couple more close calls, we realize we should practice with beacons, too. Sometimes it takes the death of a friend or an acquaintance before we realize that maybe we should study a book like this one or take an avalanche-awareness class.

That's the way almost everyone learns about avalanches. I certainly did. But don't be like me. There's standing room only in the Dumb Mistakes Club.

Photo I-4. Fifteen years ago snowmobilers could only rarely access avalanche terrain right after storms, but modern snowmobilers can go nearly any place a skier or climber can go, and in a day they can cover nearly 100 times the amount of terrain as human-powered recreationists can cover. Consequently, snowmobiler avalanche fatalities have skyrocketed in recent years. © Dan Gardiner

WILL THIS BOOK SAVE LIVES? THAT DEPENDS ON YOU

When safety measures are introduced, they usually work—but not nearly as well as could be hoped. Why? One important reason is what is known as "risk homeostasis." We all have a comfort level when it comes to risk—too much and we're scared, too little and we're bored. So when an activity is made safer through one of the "triple Es"—education, engineering, and enforcement—we often respond by simply raising our level of risk back to our comfort level, which can partially negate our advances in safety. We usually accomplish this by choosing more dangerous terrain or more dangerous snowpack, or by taking more runs. In other words, we're having more fun.

In the field of economics, this is known as the "utility." As an example, when we added seat belts, air bags, safer cars, and safer highways (engineering), then added stiff penalties for driving without a fastened seat belt (enforcement), yes, the number of fatalities per mile driven decreased slightly. But at the same time people also drove faster, farther, and crazier. According to the National Highway Traffic Safety Administration, since 1965, fatalities per capita have decreased by 44 percent while the number of miles driven per capita has increased by 106 percent. In other words, we got a double benefit: we get to drive more miles and be safer at the same time. But in looking at those numbers it's also tempting to conclude that people chose mobility (and fun) over safety two to one.

In the avalanche world we have anecdotally noticed the same trends as in the automobile example, although we lack good statistics to prove it. As backcountry travelers become more educated and use better rescue equipment, we expect a decrease in the number of avalanche fatalities per day and an increase in the number of people enjoying a lot more powder.

In other words, knowledge is safety. Knowledge is powder.

Don't go back out into the backcountry until you finish reading this book and practice with what you've learned. It will save on gray hairs, lost equipment, lost pride, hospital bills, tears shed at the funerals of friends, or devastation in the lives of your loved ones. You will also have more fun.

A NOTE ABOUT SAFETY

Safety is an important concern in all outdoor activities. No book can alert you to every hazard or anticipate the limitations of every reader. The descriptions of techniques and procedures in this book are intended to provide general information. This is not a complete text on avalanche technique. Nothing substitutes for formal instruction, routine practice, and plenty of experience. When you follow any of the procedures described here, you assume responsibility for your own safety. Use this book as a general guide to further information. Under normal conditions, excursions into the backcountry require attention to traffic, road and trail conditions, weather, terrain, the capabilities of your party, and other factors. Keeping informed on current conditions and exercising common sense are the keys to a safe, enjoyable outing.

—*Mountaineers Books*

CHAPTER 1

HOW DANGEROUS IS THE BRAIN?

Overconfidence arises because people are often blind to their own blindness.
—Daniel Kahneman,
Thinking, Fast and Slow

❖ ❖ ❖

To have a reasonably long career recreating regularly in avalanche terrain, we need to come home each day without an injury or accident for somewhere around 99.99 percent of the time. That's a lot of perfection. Yet as we all know, people are not perfect.

At least in Utah, about a third of avalanche victims who died in avalanches did so because they lacked knowledge and bumbled into an obviously dangerous situation. However, two-thirds had at least some avalanche training and knowledge; some even had a lot of snow savvy. In almost all avalanche accidents involving avalanche-educated victims, they (1) failed to notice obvious clues to instability, (2) overestimated their ability to deal with the risk, or (3) realized the danger but proceeded anyway.

In other words, smart people often do stupid things. And yes, that includes me on an all-too-regular basis, as my wife would be happy to tell you. And by extension, that means you—yes, *you*—probably also do stupid things, and fairly regularly, I'm guessing. Since we all do stupid things, let's just have a group hug and talk about it.

From what I regularly see on any sunny Saturday with the lure of powder snow, when people are free to exercise their American ideals of freedom and liberty, they all too often demonstrate why they shouldn't.

On those sunny Saturdays, with the combination of avalanche danger and powder snow, sometimes I go out with my camera and document the madness. Other times I stay home because I just can't face it, and I leave my phone on so I can field the flood of requests for media interviews after the inevitable accident reports start crackling over the scanners.

Photo1-1. A snowmobiler found the trigger point of this avalanche after his party tracked up the entire slope. Luckily, he was not caught.

In the Utah backcountry, we have the worst imaginable situation: two million people live directly at the base of a large, steep mountain range with easy access to dangerous, uncontrolled avalanche terrain, all just a 15-minute drive from town. I see all kinds of people flooding into the backcountry—snowmobilers, skiers, snowboarders, snowshoers, hikers, runners—ranging in skills from Boy Scout troops and church groups to hard-core athletes with their film crews.

I regularly see people breaking all the rules laid out in this book. People jump onto a slope immediately above one another and recreate with multiple people on the slope at the same time. People build jumps in narrow, terrain-trap gullies. One group races another group for the top of a powder slope, all bristling with video cameras on their helmets as they film from midslope. Many people are without even basic rescue gear. Many others know the risks but go anyway.

You get the picture.

I refer to these days as mass hysteria. All the broken rules mentioned above are on prominent display.

Why do smart people sometimes do stupid things? Many refer to this subject as human factors, which usually include time and money constraints, equipment, travel skills, communication, and weather. But I think the most important human factors (and the hardest to mitigate) are *heuristic traps* and *cognitive biases*. Daniel Kahneman's 2011 book, *Thinking, Fast and Slow,* a *New York Times* bestseller, should also be required reading after you finish this book. Kahneman won the Nobel Prize in economics, and he is one of the world's leading authorities on the psychology of decision making.

TAKE-HOME POINT

Both our intuitive brain and our logical brain are commonly fooled by a number of biases and mental shortcuts.

Kahneman introduces a useful concept: The brain has two systems for making decisions—the intuitive brain and the logical brain—which he calls System 1 and System 2. The intuitive brain makes quick, efficient decisions mostly based on pattern recognition. Our logical brain is called upon when heavier lifting is required—something more complex than a snap judgment. The logical brain is slower and lazier, but it can overrule some of the quirks of the intuitive brain. Both the intuitive brain and the logical brain can yield both good and bad decisions.

Like most human traits, biases and mental shortcuts (also known as "heuristics") are both good and bad. We could not operate in our daily lives without them because they help us make rapid decisions. For instance, how long would it take you to buy groceries if you had to read every label and research every product? Marketing departments exploit this to their advantage, and clever advertising affects all of us whether we realize it or not. In the game of avalanche risk, we have a number of biases and mental shortcuts that commonly fool even the pros. Below, in roughly the order of occurrence we witness most often in avalanche accidents, I list some of the more important ones from Kahneman's book as well as some that I have noticed.

Herding: Also called "groupthink." We take more risks when we are in a larger group or when we are following the crowd. All species of animals do this. Like wildebeests crossing a crocodile-infested river, if one person gets away with jumping onto a risky avalanche slope, others follow. I use the term herding to encompass several mental shortcuts described by others under different names such as "risky shift" (when we're in larger groups we take more risks), "acceptance" (we take cues from others), and "social facilitation" (we take more risks when we're trying to impress others).

Competition: We take more risks when we are competing for powder, to get noticed, or to impress mates.

Familiarity: We feel more comfortable and take more risks in familiar environments.

Expert halo: We tend to follow someone, without question, who is an "expert" (for instance, someone who knows the route or is very skilled in a particular sport), even though that person may not have very good avalanche skills.

Loss aversion, or sunk costs: "We came all this way. We're not turning back now. All we have to do is get to that pass over there and we're home free."

Substitution: We tend to answer an easy question instead of ask the hard one. For example, "I'm in a good mood and it's a sunny day, so that slope couldn't be dangerous."

WYSIATI (What You See Is All There Is): For example, "It's safe here in the trees, so it must be safe up there on the ridge too."

Confirmation bias: Once we've formed a belief, we tend to rationalize away conflicting information. "That's my decision, so don't confuse me with the facts."

Goal blindness: Once we've focused on a goal, we tend to be blind to alternatives. For example, "We came here to film a sick line, so I'm not going down that boring way." (A better approach: Make the journey the destination.)

Bias of confidence over doubt: We express confidence much more often than we express doubt—even without a good reason. (Kahneman calls this the Engine of Capitalism.) "I'm not exactly sure where we are, but hey, we're making great time."

Anchors: We latch on to one fact and anchor our assumptions to it. For example, "The avalanche report said low danger, so that avalanche over there must be a fluke."

Illusions of skill: We often attribute random events to skill (a common mistake made in stock trading). Snow is stable 95 percent of the time, but we mistake lack of avalanches for our having made good decisions.

Cognitive illusions: One cognitive illusion is that we have a poor understanding of probability. We overestimate the occurrence of small events, like 10 percent chance of snow, and underestimate the likelihood of large-magnitude events, like avalanches.

Hindsight bias: When we look backward in time, random events can appear to have meaning and pattern (this is the basis for conspiracy theories). "How could those people be such idiots? They should have known that the weather forecasts around here are always wrong."

Regression to the mean: We are often fooled by randomness. Both high and low results are likely to be closer to average next time. (Sportscasters often invent reasons why one good performance is not followed by an equally good performance.)

Law of small numbers: We forget that a small sample size will produce poor conclusions. For example, "I've ridden this slope 10 times and I've never seen it slide."

Planning fallacy: We forget that projects (like writing this book) always take longer than expected.

Cognitive ease: A political sound bite or an advertising slogan may make sense as long as we don't think about it too much or check the facts.

This list goes on and on. . . . Read some of the books listed in Resources at the back of this book for more details.

Yet we really need to use both the intuitive brain *and* the logical brain in order to make good decisions. People highly skilled and experienced in their area of expertise get very good at seamlessly delegating tasks to the appropriate part of the brain and coming up with good decisions. For example, a nurse might think, "This patient doesn't look right. I need to study his chart and see if we're missing something."

THE INTUITIVE BRAIN

I cringe every time I hear someone say, "Just trust your gut," because, as usual, whether you can trust your gut depends on several things. As many researchers have shown, you can trust your intuition only if both of these are true:

1. You developed your intuition in a relatively instant-feedback environment.
2. You have a lot of experience.

Instant Feedback versus Poor Feedback

In an instant-feedback environment, feedback occurs within about a day or less of your having made the decision. Examples of people who make decisions in an instant-feedback environment include chess or video game players, emergency room doctors, firefighters, weather forecasters—and, yes, avalanche forecasters.

As I often tell avalanche students, by far the best way to learn about avalanches is to get a job on a ski patrol and perform avalanche control with explosives on a regular basis. With every storm, you go out with a pack full of explosives and conduct dozens of trial-and-error experiments in a relatively controlled environment. With every big wallop from an explosive, variables in the snowpack, weather, and terrain are instantly linked in your mind with avalanche activity. In addition, you do this activity regularly. Especially if it is combined with mentoring from the wiser old dogs, doing avalanche control with explosives is a great example of an instant-feedback environment in which you learn very quickly.

A poor feedback environment is one in which you don't find out if your decision was right or wrong for perhaps a month or a year or longer. Examples of people who make decisions in a poor feedback environment include mutual fund managers, economists, preventive medicine doctors, or pundits who predict trends in the future, whether political, world event, or technological trends. Research has repeatedly shown that the success rate in poor-feedback endeavors is quite low—at best, only marginally better than flipping a coin.

If that's not enough, this type of intuition tends to be accompanied by overconfidence and extreme choices. In other words, all too often this type of decision maker when wrong tends to be confidently and spectacularly wrong.

Learning about avalanches on your own in the backcountry—the school of hard knocks—is a particularly cruel environment in which to learn. It's a poor-feedback environment. Since snow is stable about 95 percent of the time, you get a lot of positive reinforcement even if you make poor decisions. In addition, only about one out of three people who unintentionally trigger avalanches is caught in one.

It's like a slot machine in which the quarters jingle into your cup 59 out of 60 times. Yes! Nothing like success! Then on the 60th pull, two big goons throw a gunny sack over your head and beat you with baseball bats, charge your credit card $10,000, and throw you into the street. After you stagger to your feet, stumble home, and think it over for a few days, you convince yourself that it *must* have been a fluke. "I was winning every time," you tell yourself. "Those goons were a fluke." With trepidation, you tiptoe back to the machine, pull the handle again, and, sure enough, the quarters start jingling. Yippee! Then, eventually, it's the goons and the baseball bats again. It takes a lot of pulls on the slot machine handle for us to learn the downside of the game, and with avalanches sometimes we don't survive the lesson.

So if people learned about avalanches in a poor-feedback environment—say by traveling on their own in the backcountry without a mentor and only rarely experiencing dicey avalanche conditions—"trusting their gut" (their intuitive brain) is probably the worst thing they can do. Not only have they been habituated into making poor decisions on the days they've jumped onto avalanche-prone slopes and gotten away with it, but often the intuition they acquired along the way is faulty or biased.

When you don't have that ideal job as an avalanche control worker, you need to seek out instant-feedback environments: Don't stay home on high danger days; go out and wallow in it—but do it in low-consequence terrain. Find a small test slope, like a road cut or small slope where the wind is rapidly drifting snow onto a steep, 3-meter (10-foot) high slope. Jump onto this small slope to see how it responds. Remember to do it with a partner in case the results are more serious than expected. If that small test slope doesn't avalanche, find another one, perhaps on another aspect, that will.

When you find a slope that responds, notice where it breaks. Dig down on the crown face or flank and memorize the structure of the snow. Take a close look at the weak layer. Do many different kinds of stability tests so you can experience "quality 1 shear," when the slab jumps out like a spring-loaded cash register drawer (see How Avalanches Work in Chapter 3). Notice its aspect, which direction it faces, and other features around it. Then find another test slope and another. Spend a few hours reveling in the greatest gift for instant-feedback learning: unstable conditions in safe terrain. Repeat often. But remember, do this only on very low-consequence slopes; it's much like first learning to ride a bike; you start slowly and on a grassy sward, not above a cliff.

How Much Experience Is Enough?

They say it takes 10,000 hours of experience in an instant-feedback environment to master a complex skill, and avalanches are no exception. Ten thousand hours is five hours per day for six years, which is a lot of time. But in my experience, you're not an avalanche expert until you have at least 10,000 hours under your belt in a good learning environment.

I don't consider people to be true experts until I see some humility too. This might mean backing off of a sweet line because you know that a slope is guilty until proven innocent and you just don't have enough evidence yet. True experts also show fear and respect, as they realize that the world is a much more random place than they imagined, and what they previously thought was skill was mostly luck. The sidebar "Evolution of an Avalanche Expert" illustrates this journey to avalanche expertise.

So what does all this mean? It means that especially if we don't have a lot of experience in instant-feedback environments, we have to be very, very careful about "trusting our gut" because of the dozens of different delusions and illusions that our brain can produce (see the list of biases and mental shortcuts at the start of this chapter). Intuition, especially intuition not gained by a lot of experience in a high-feedback environment, can be strongly affected by biases—resulting in great potential danger if that is the only kind of thinking we use in decision making.

EVOLUTION OF AN AVALANCHE EXPERT

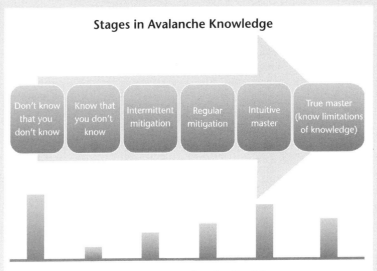

This is my conceptual view of the journey to becoming an avalanche expert. In the ignorance-is-bliss stage, we don't know that we don't know, and our confidence is at an all-time high. A disproportionate number of avalanche accidents occur to this group. Often during our first avalanche class, we realize the dangers and what idiots we've been. All too clearly, we now know that we don't know. Our confidence drops to an all-time low. Then we begin our slow journey to learn about avalanches, and our confidence slowly rises as we mitigate our experience, that is, adapting and adjusting, until, after several years of regular experience in an instant-feedback environment, we learn to make good, intuitive decisions. We are now intuitive masters. But the mark of a true avalanche master is realizing the limitations of our knowledge and our susceptibility to biases and mental shortcuts, and acknowledging that the world is a much more random place than we would like to believe. True avalanche masters cycle back to the know-that-you-don't-know stage and once again see the world with a beginner's mind. They show humility, fear, suspicion, and an insatiable curiosity and respect for what they don't yet know. You will often see them in conservative terrain when others are letting it all hang out on higher-risk slopes.

THE LOGICAL BRAIN

Our brain uses intuition whenever it can because doing so is so much faster and more efficient. The logical brain has been called lazy because it takes energy to rev it up, so we often use intuition when we should use logic. This has been called "substitution." When asked a hard question, we substitute an easy question in its place and call the answer good. (For example: "Would this man make a good president? Hmmm. He has a square jaw and acts confident. Yes, I'm convinced he would make a great president.")

For instance, as I mentioned before, very few mutual fund managers can consistently beat the market year after year, most pundits make predictions that have almost no correlation to actual events, and many Fortune 500 CEOs are paid salaries that are largely unwarranted. Yet, when confronted with the facts, most of these highly paid professionals just shrug it off because they would rather believe a narrative ("I wouldn't get paid this much if I wasn't good.") than statistics. This is called the "narrative fallacy."

It means that Moses was right. Humans are a damned mess. We need rules!

Even pros are affected by competition, familiarity, or the other biases talked about at the start of this chapter, as evidenced by occasional close calls and fatalities. In almost all of these cases, using something as simple as a checklist would have prevented the accident. In other words, we all need to be prompted, even forced, to use our logical brains. Therefore, we all need to follow a system.

WHAT'S THE ANSWER? FOLLOWING A SYSTEM

It is my belief, having learned from 35 years in the avalanche business, that we can operate safely in dangerous avalanche terrain only by operating under a tightly controlled system. *The system is the solution.*

Examples of successful systems include those used by reputable, tightly controlled and disciplined professional operations such as ski patrols doing regular avalanche control and helicopter guiding companies or mountain guide operations who regularly and safely take people into potentially dangerous terrain.

Below are several systems that have proven to be effective in other fields. None of them are magic bullets, but little things that when done reliably really add up. They are the layers in our safety net system, comprising a strong, reproducible system to help us avoid dumb mistakes.

Checklists, Procedures, and Decision-Making Aids

Countless studies have shown that even simple decision-making aids and checklists can engage the logical brain and can produce dramatically better decisions. And even among highly skilled people, a checklist can help "prime" us for conditions we might encounter in the task at hand. For these reasons, many industries have gravitated toward checklists and computer algorithms. Airplane pilots were one of the first groups to use them, and these tools have now spread through most other industries, such as the military, firefighters, the business world, the financial sector, and the medical profession. The transition has been only reluctantly accepted in some industries mainly because we humans don't want to believe that a simple checklist, as opposed to years of experience or training, can consistently help us make better decisions. But such systems can.

In this book of avalanche essentials, I present simplified checklists and decision-making aids. While these aids certainly don't catch all the subtleties and complexities of avalanches, they work in most common scenarios we encounter in avalanche terrain, and they will help you travel more safely and have more fun in avalanche terrain. Yet there often is a trade-off between accuracy and utility. Long checklists or complex decision-making aids may be more accurate and thorough, but fewer people will use them. Simple is almost always better because they get used. Shorter checklists work; you'll find them in this book. For an engaging discussion on the importance of checklists, see *The Checklist Manifesto: How to Get Things Right* by Atul Gawande.

A Ulysses Contract

Perhaps you remember the story of Ulysses when he returned from the Trojan War. He and his crew were sailing near the island of Siren, where beautiful singing voices had lured countless ships to sail too close and founder on the rocks, killing all aboard. Ulysses wanted to hear the music but also survive the experience. So he instructed his crew to put beeswax in their ears, then lash Ulysses to the mast and sail past the island. Most important, they were instructed to keep to their course no matter what Ulysses might order them to do.

This kind of ironclad agreement is known as a Ulysses Contract: once you agree to a course of action, you also agree to never, under any circumstances, change the safety plan. Heliski guides do this by making a run list in the morning consisting of green-light, yellow-light, and red-light slopes. Their Ulysses Contract is to ski only the green-light slopes. As they gather more information during the day, they can meet and then, only after careful evaluation, decide to move into some of the yellow-light slopes. But they never touch the red-light slopes. Period. This way, no one is tempted by the euphoria of the day, pressure from the clients, or any other biases or mental shortcuts.

I practice a similar Ulysses Contract on an almost daily basis. If I know there's a particularly nasty weak layer buried in the snowpack (a monster in the basement), I make an agreement with myself either to avoid the terrain where the monsters live or, if I am in monster habitat, to never get on a slope steeper than 30 degrees (including locally connected terrain; see Chapter 2, How Dangerous Is the Terrain?).

A Premortem

Most of us have heard of a postmortem, a report written after someone has died that analyzes the facts and decisions that led up to the death. But what is a premortem? As we all know, hindsight is 20-20, so in a premortem we simply turn the arrow of time around so we can see more clearly into the future. In other words, we imagine how the story will play on the evening news or what our friends will say at our funeral. This technique often identifies most of the reasons why we might be wrong. All too often, we don't ask ourselves until it's too late. Doing a premortem has been suggested by a number of experts on decision making as an effective way to keep unwarranted optimism in check. (The optimism bias seems to be hard-wired into the human brain.)

I have done premortems for many years. Since I'm considered to be an avalanche expert (except by the avalanches), I'm more motivated than most to think these second-guessing thoughts. The embarrassment alone would kill me. The regular practice of performing premortems has definitely kept me out of trouble many times. I also find it helpful to imagine what my boss would say: "Now, let me get this straight..."

A Dissenting Opinion

Along the same lines as asking *yourself* why you might be wrong is asking someone *else* for a dissenting opinion. Another term for this might be looking for a devil's advocate.

The origin of the term "devil's advocate" dates back to AD 1587 when the Roman Catholic Church held hearings to determine whether a particularly saintly person deserved to be canonized. The group that supported the canonization were "God's advocates," and the Pope began the practice of appointing a lawyer known as the "Devil's advocate" whose job it was to present the skeptical view and identify holes in the prevailing arguments. In other words, the church invented a system to force consideration of both sides of an argument instead of being swayed by groupthink. It makes sense that clergy—who presumably know more about myriad human foibles than most—were early adopters of this solution.

For the same reason, many years ago the US Supreme Court began the policy of issuing a dissenting opinion for every major decision. In my family, my grandfather, mother, brother, uncle, and a cousin were lawyers, so we had nightly debates

Photo 1-2. A skier-triggered soft slab avalanche in which the victim was uninjured. The victim or someone in the victim's party triggers 93 percent of avalanche accidents, making avalanches the only natural hazard usually triggered by the victim. This is good news because it means we can prevent most avalanche fatalities by mastering avalanche and decision-making skills.

around the dinner table in which someone always jumped in to play the devil's advocate. I grew up thinking that everyone debated issues this way, though I quickly learned that many of my friends did not take kindly to the same tactic. It's best, I found, to explain what you are doing first.

So how do you do this in a group? Most of us agree that going against group consensus is a delicate task. It's easier to bring up differing opinions in a small group of friends out for the day, especially if you take the time to negotiate the plan and goals on the phone before the trip and in the car on the way to the trailhead. (Remember, explain the concept of devil's advocate first.) Be sure to have your discussions in the planning and commuting stages, because it's much harder to communicate when you're spread out, huffing, and puffing up the hill or zooming along on snowmobiles. Once the group is underway, I find it's best to use preplanned spots where you regroup and discuss the next step. Watch out for times when the fastest travelers bolt to the front, and the slowest members never get the chance to catch up and discuss their concerns (a scenario known as "the accordion").

Introducing a dissenting opinion in larger groups is among the most difficult tasks any of us ever face. Before each expedition or major outing, I usually play the safety nerd and give a little speech to launch a discussion of the goals of the trip (my goals are always to come home safe and as better friends than we were before the trip). On the multiday trip, I try to operate like a good guiding company would, including quick morning and evening meetings to discuss plans and options in which we are free to work out differing expectations and goals.

The worst situations involve a larger group of casual acquaintances in which there is little organization, communication, or structure—in other words, the groups involved in most backcountry outings. I almost always avoid groups of more than four people unless my goal is a day of socializing, in which case the group needs to choose very conservative terrain because of all the extra hazards from human factors. (See Photo 1-2.)

YOUR PERSONAL DISASTER FACTORS

Imagine a time when you had a close call or some sort of disaster. Then think about the human factors that led to the bad decision. This is a list of your personal disaster factors.

It seems that each person has an individual subset of personal disaster factors. In other words, you don't necessarily have to scroll through the complete checklist of biases each time you make a decision; instead, concentrate first on your own personal disaster factor biases.

My friend Ian McCammon has used this technique in his avalanche classes, and I think it works well. When I do the exercise myself, I find that most of my bone-headed mistakes were caused by haste. I tend to be impatient and ambitious and always try to bite off more than I can chew. Because I'm always in a hurry, I some-times cut corners, which gets me in trouble. I have to regularly work on schooling my patience. Whenever I find myself in an impatient, corner-cutting mood, I try to tone it back to a safe level.

Try to develop your own list of personal disaster factors, as well as some of the other logical-brain techniques described in this chapter.

CHAPTER 2

HOW DANGEROUS IS THE TERRAIN?

If you're going to learn nothing else about avalanches, learn how to read and manage avalanche terrain. The snowpack is fickle and weather is even more fickle (both are covered in Chapters 3 and 4), and people are most fickle of all (described in Chapter 1). In this swirling fog of uncertainty, however, we have a reliable, faithful, and unchanging friend: terrain. The only way to live a long, happy life in the mountains is to master the basics of managing terrain based on snow, weather, and people. When snowpack, weather, or people are the question—terrain is always the answer.

THE FIVE As AND TWO Cs

Many instructors teach avalanche terrain using the Five As and Two Cs, and here is my version:

- ❖ Angle: steepness of the slope
- ❖ Anchors versus obstacles
- ❖ Aspect—wind: how the slope is affected by wind
- ❖ Aspect—sun: how the slope is affected by the sun
- ❖ Altitude
- ❖ Consequences: what will happen if a slope slides
- ❖ Complexity: the amount of avalanche terrain and how committing it is

Note: Some people use appearance (shape) as one of the Five As, but as I explain later in this chapter, shape is mostly about steepness (angle) and consequences.

I have listed these seven elements of terrain considerations roughly in the order of their importance. This chapter discusses each of them one by one.

ANGLE: STEEPNESS OF THE SLOPE

Gravity never sleeps. The steeper the slope, the more that objects, including snow, want to slide off it—but avalanche *danger* doesn't necessarily work that way. The

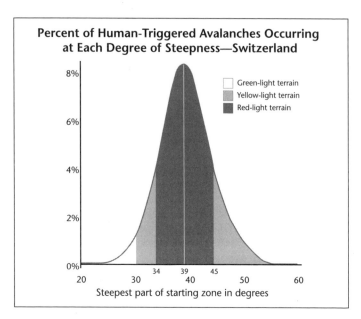

Figure 2-1. In this graph of the starting-zone steepness of 995 human-triggered avalanches, I have separated the steepness into red-light, yellow-light and green-light zones based on what seem like critical dividing lines from my experience. The very steep slopes can never be green light because of regular sluffs and other hazards of very steep slopes. (From *Lawinenkunde*, by Harvey, Rhymer, and Schweizer)

danger that an avalanche will occur increases with increasing slope steepness until about 38–39 degrees of angle. Then—counterintuitively—danger actually *decreases* as the slope steepens. That's because sluffs and smaller slabs run more frequently on steeper slopes, releasing snow (weight) from the slope, which significantly reduces buildup on deeper, more dangerous slabs. This tendency does not mean that large slab avalanches don't occur on 60-degree slopes, because they certainly do. It just means that they occur much less commonly than on 40-degree slopes. See Figure 2-1.

In the steepness graph (Figure 2-1), the bull's-eye steepness is 39 degrees; nearly three out of four avalanches occur in red-light starting zones (34 to 45 degrees), 10% occur in the yellow-light terrain on the gentle side of the curve (30-34 degrees), 13% on the steep end of the curve, and only 3% on slopes less than 30 degrees.

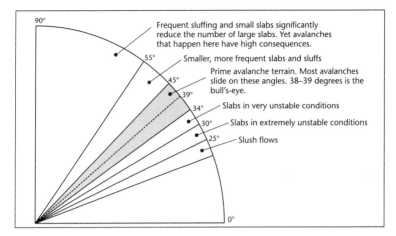

Figure 2-2. Three out of four avalanches occur on slopes between 34 and 45 degrees.

TAKE-HOME POINT

Avalanches are extremely sensitive to slope steepness. Thirty degrees is barely steep enough to slide, yet avalanche activity reaches a maximum at 38–39 degrees of slope angle. This difference of only 8 to 9 degrees doesn't seem like much to humans, but it's monumentally important to avalanches. (See Figure 2-2.)

Caveat: Your situation may vary. Avalanches tend to occur on steeper slopes in maritime climates—where the median is around 40–41 degrees—because wet snow and nonpersistent weak layers (persistent weak layers are more common in continental climates, nonpersistent in maritime climates) tend to slide on steeper slopes (Figure 2-3). Also, with surface hoar as the weak layer (see How Avalanches Work in Chapter 3), the median steepness is gentler—36 degrees. The bottom line is that you should treat these statistics for slope steepness with some leeway for several reasons:

1. It's difficult to measure slope steepness, so these steepness numbers are a bit squishy.
2. All avalanche bed surfaces exhibit a range of steepness; a single number never tells the whole story.
3. Steepness varies somewhat by climate.
4. Steepness varies somewhat by weak layer.

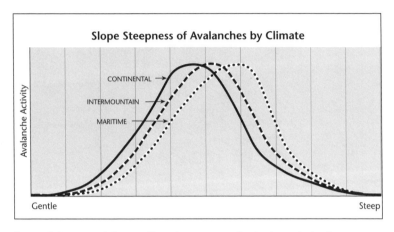

Figure 2-3. A conceptual diagram of how slope steepness of avalanches varies by climate

Note: Avalanche professionals used to think that avalanches ran on gentler slopes during very unstable conditions, but recent research from Switzerland indicates otherwise. Avalanches just *seem* to run on gentler slopes during conditions of high and extreme danger because the bigger avalanches triggered in these conditions can run farther into flat terrain and because, as instability rises, it's easier to trigger avalanches from a distance (called "remote triggers"). For instance, you can collapse a weak layer on a gentle slope, which propagates to a locally connected steeper slope. (See below for more details.)

"Cool," you say. "After storms, just avoid slopes between those critical slope angles." Yet those are *exactly* the slopes we like to recreate on. In knee-deep fresh powder, on skis or a snowboard, you need to be on a 35-degree slope just to get going, and 38 degrees is ideal for most snow sports, including climbing on a snowmobile.

Good News—Bad News

The good news is that most avalanches occur within a narrow range of slope steepness. The bad news is that those slopes are exactly where most of us like to recreate. Slopes between 34 and 45 degrees cause the vast majority of avalanche fatalities, as shown in Figure 2-1.

Table 2-1 illustrates the relationship between steepness and avalanche danger, as well as the perception of danger by most recreationists.

TABLE 2-1	AVALANCHE DANGER BY STEEPNESS OF SLOPE		
Steepness	Slope Rating at a Ski Area	Avalanche Activity	Perception of Danger
Up to 11°	Beginner to intermediate slopes (green slopes)	Slush flows in arctic climates. Infrequent wet avalanche run outs. Dry slabs in extremely unusual situations.	"What is this, a golf course?"
11°–25°	Intermediate slopes (blue slopes)	Infrequent slabs in very unstable conditions	"OK, but not steep enough for having fun."
25°–35°	Advanced slopes (black diamond)	Slabs increasing rapidly in frequency above 30°	"This is starting to get steep enough to have fun."
Undefined but generally 35° and steeper	Expert-only slopes (double black diamond)	Prime avalanche terrain; bull's-eye around 38° or 39°. Frequent slab avalanches.	"Perfect!" But this is where most avalanches happen.
45°–55°	Extreme terrain (couloirs in cliffs— usually roped off)	Frequent smaller slabs and sluffs reduce the number of larger slabs	"Whoa, this is seriously steep. I'm scared."
55°–90°	Alpine climbing terrain (cliffs and very steep couloirs)	Frequent sluffs and small slabs dramatically reduce the number of larger slabs	"Wow, it's a cliff. Give me a rope."

Note: In my experience, most novices overestimate slope steepness by at least 5 degrees; they'll tell you they just snowboarded a 40-degree slope that upon measurement is only 35 degrees. To guard against that tendency, learn to accurately measure a slope's steepness.

Using an Inclinometer

Yep, that's right: You need to measure the slope, and an inclinometer is your best tool. I've taught countless avalanche classes, and I've come to the conclusion that people are not only appalling judges of slope steepness, but they're not very accurate at measuring them either.

Some avalanche educators say that if you're going to carry only one avalanche prediction tool, an inclinometer—which measures the steepness of a slope—should be it. Luckily, you have many choices.

Inclinometer apps: My favorite method is to use an app on my smartphone. By the time you read this, there will probably be 30 choices of such apps. Most that I have seen not only measure steepness but also give the aspect (direction the slope faces), altitude (elevation), latitude, and longitude, which also saves

Figure 2-4. This popular backcountry skiing slope is tricky because the upper third is gentler with many sections less than 30 degrees but the lower section rolls over into terrain at prime steepness—35–40 degrees. Plus, there are many trees to hit on the way down if you're caught. Many people have fun working the gentler slopes in the upper part but they get into trouble when they descend too far or use the entire slope as their descent run at the end of the day. The avalanche in this photo killed an experienced backcountry skier. Most of these avalanche paths end in a creek bottom, which is a sharp terrain trap.

you from carrying several other gizmos, such as a compass, a GPS device, and an altitude watch. How cool is that? Remember that you have to first calibrate your smartphone: Lay it on a flat countertop and zero out the steepness. We'll learn more about these factors in Chapter 3, How Dangerous Is the Snowpack?

Compass or card inclinometer: Another good choice is a relatively inexpensive compass that also has a plumb-bob inclinometer. Avalanche safety supply companies also distribute a small, inexpensive inclinometer card that uses a string as a plumb bob. Either works fairly well, but I figure if you need a compass anyway, you might as well get one with an inclinometer.

Some avalanche books recommend laying a ski pole on the slope and setting the inclinometer on top of the ski pole to measure the slope angle. But the ski pole method is notoriously inaccurate not only because of factors like a bent ski pole

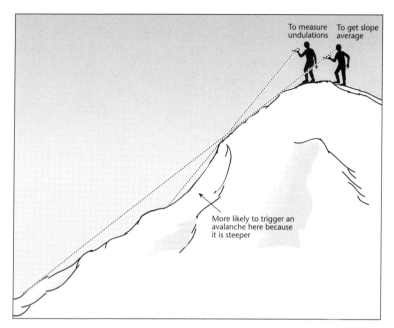

Figure 2-5. With an inclinometer, the most accurate measurement is to simply sight along the tangent of the slope either from the top or the bottom. Local measurements of steepness (such as are obtained by using a ski pole) are less accurate because you measure small variations in the snow surface instead of the average steepness.

or the difficulty of getting a pole to lie flat to the slope, but because this method measures only a very small area. The best way is to sight up or down the slope with the inclinometer, because you can average out all the small undulations that fool the ski pole method (Figure 2-5). Try to average a 10 meter by 10 meter section of slope.

TAKE-HOME POINT

Without training and instant feedback, humans are poor judges of slope steepness. Learn how to use an inclinometer until you have calibrated your avalanche eyeballs. This is probably the most important avalanche skill to develop.

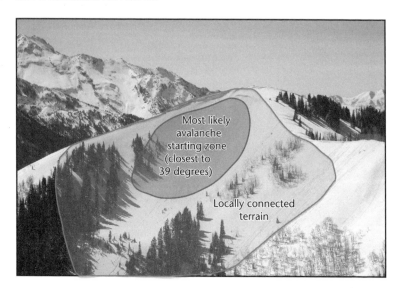

Figure 2-6. When traveling in avalanche terrain, it's essential to consider "locally connected terrain." Although the part of the slope closest to 39 degrees will control whether the slope avalanches or not, it's common to trigger avalanches from gentler or steeper terrain by collapsing the weak layer. In very unstable conditions, the resulting avalanche can often pull other parts of the slope along with it. It's especially dangerous to trigger the slope from the bottom because everything comes down on top of you, often resulting in a very deep burial. Also remember that it's also possible to trigger an avalanche from the flat parts of the ridge above, which can be pulled along with the avalanche as well, like a tablecloth pulled by a child.

What Is the Slope Connected To?

You don't have to be on a steep slope to trigger it; a person can trigger an avalanche from a distance. We call these "remote" triggers. Especially in very unstable conditions with a persistent weak layer, it's common for people to unwittingly trigger steep slopes from an adjacent connected slope, especially from the bottom. In extreme conditions, fractures can propagate long distances, but in most cases you need to pay attention to terrain that I call "locally connected" to steeper terrain nearby (Figure 2-6). Remote triggers are common in the following circumstances:

❖ You can trigger avalanches remotely, especially when avalanche danger is high or extreme, combined with a persistent weak layer (see Chapters 3 and 4).

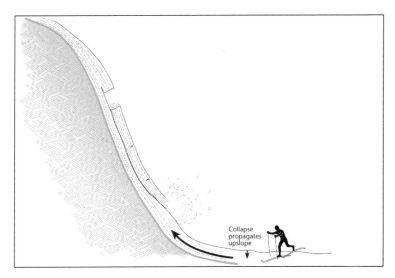

Figure 2-7. Especially in very unstable conditions, you can trigger an avalanche nearly as easily from the bottom as from the slope itself.

Figure 2-8. Especially in very unstable conditions combined with a hard slab, it's possible to trigger the avalanche while standing on a flat ridge above the slope. Sometimes the resulting avalanche can pull that slab along for the ride, like a child breaking the dishes by pulling on the tablecloth.

❖ You can trigger a steep slope above by crossing a gentle or flat slope below nearly as easily as crossing the steep slope itself (Figure 2-7). Fractures can propagate long distances across flat slopes.

❖ You can trigger avalanches below you from a flatter slope and especially from a ridge top, as shown in Figure 2-8. In extreme conditions, especially with thick, hard slabs, victims have been pulled off flat ridges this way—like when a child grabs onto the edge of a tablecloth and pulls all the dishes down onto the floor.

❖ You can trigger an adjacent slope. The slope you are standing on might not be steep enough to slide on its own, but an avalanche on an adjacent steeper slope might pull your slope along for the ride.

Note on Slope Shape (Appearance)

Most avalanche books and classes have taught that avalanches occur more commonly on convex slopes, and therefore are more dangerous. From my observations, slope shape is not nearly as important as steepness—the closer to 39 degrees, the more dangerous—regardless of shape. Indeed, studies in recent years have come to different conclusions; some find human-triggered avalanches to be slightly more common on convex slopes, while another study found them far more common on planar or concave slopes. The bottom line is that I like to focus on the basics of steepness and consequences instead of on the shape of the slope.

ANCHORS VERSUS OBSTACLES

Anchors such as trees, rocks, and bushes help to hold a snow slab in place. However, anchors if sparse can also be dangerous, because if they don't help to hold a slab in place, they suddenly become obstacles to hit on the way down. Here are some key points regarding anchors versus obstacles.

❖ Anchors must be densely spaced to be effective. People often misunderstand this essential point. Sparse anchors, also known as "false anchors," especially when combined with a soft slab, have very little effect and therefore become dangerous obstacles that you will hit on the way down. When anchors are not thickly spaced enough to hold a slab in place, they suddenly become giant baseball bats that can beat us to death while we slide through them at freeway speeds. As you travel from thick trees into sparse trees, remember that anchors suddenly turn into possibly dangerous obstacles, and can be trigger points.

❖ Anchors that don't stick up through the weak layer have no effect (Figure 2-9). They need to penetrate well into the slab.

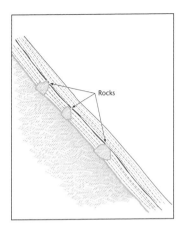

Figure 2-9. These anchors hold the lower slab in place but do nothing for the upper slab.

Figure 2-10. Evergreen trees with branches frozen in place, such as spruce and fir, are more effective than bare-trunk trees like aspen or lodgepole pine.

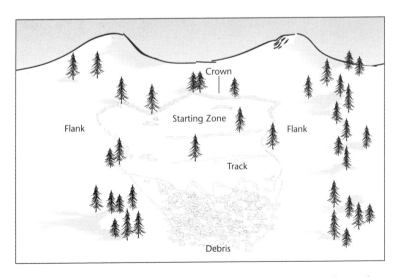

Figure 2-11. Parts of a slab avalanche. Notice that the crown and flanks tend to fracture from anchor to anchor.

❖ Spruce and fir trees with branches frozen into the slab are much more effective anchors than trees with few low branches, such as aspen or lodgepole pine (Figure 2-10). Also, the snow near trees tends to be more stable because snow falling off trees compacts the snow below and also because the trees tend to capture and re-radiate heat onto the snow surface. Note that flagged trees—trees with all the uphill branches stripped off—indicate trees that regularly get hit by avalanches.

❖ Anchors hold hard slabs in place much better than they hold soft slabs.

❖ Avalanche fracture lines tend to run from anchor to anchor because anchors are stress concentration points, rather like the perforations between sheets on a roll of paper towels. In other words, you stand a better chance of staying on the good side of a fracture line by standing above a tree instead of below it. Also, anchors tend to break up the continuity of the slab so fractures tend not to propagate as far as they would without anchors. See Figure 2-11.

Photo 2-1. If you were caught in an avalanche here, you would almost certainly hit trees and rocks on the way down. The thicker trees on the viewer's left seem like they are thick enough to be anchors, but as you can see in this photo, they were not able to hold the slab in place for the terrain above the thick trees. These anchors suddenly turned into obstacles.

Figure 2-12. Avalanche paths that terminate in trees are very dangerous. Remember that trees such as aspen are a disaster species, which recover quickly in places where avalanches or fire tend to destroy them.

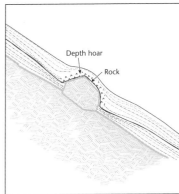

Figure 2-13. In climates with cold temperatures and a shallow snowpack, depth hoar tends to grow around rocks, making them trigger points instead of anchors.

Good News—Bad News

The good news is that when anchors are thickly spaced, they help to hold a slab in place and they are our friends.

The bad news is that if they fail to anchor the slab, your best friends suddenly turn into your worst enemies. Anchors become obstacles that will break your bones and could kill you (Figure 2-12). Remember that one out of four avalanche fatalities results from the trauma of hitting trees and rocks on the way down. Thus, trees and rocks can be either anchors or obstacles depending on how thickly spaced they are. (See the Consequences section below.)

Caveat: In continental climates—thin, cold snowpacks such as on the eastern side of the Rocky Mountains—faceted snow commonly forms around rocks near the surface. Thin snow means weak snow. Because of this, it's common to trigger avalanches while crossing near rocks that stick out of the snow or other shallow snowpack areas. Therefore, especially in continental climates, don't think of rocks as islands of safety or anchors; they can be trigger points (Figure 2-13).

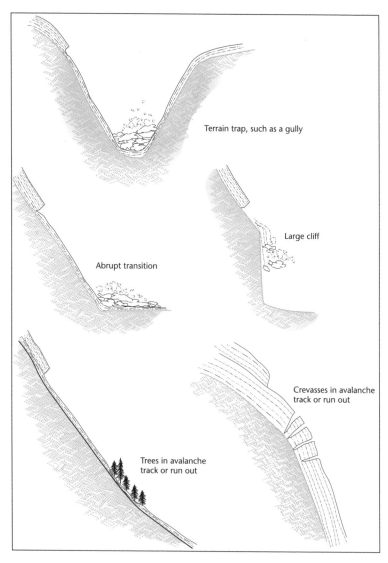

Figure 2-14. Different types of terrain with bad consequences. You should be obsessed with consequences—what will happen if it slides?

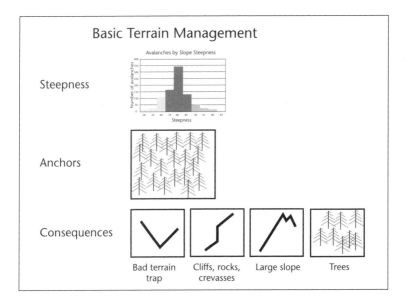

Figure 2-15. If we focus only on terrain and not snowpack variables, the danger of the terrain depends on three factors: steepness, anchors, and consequences.

CONSEQUENCES

Once we have mastered the basics of steepness and understand the significance of anchors, we can then consider consequences, which I like to teach using a standard probability-consequence diagram (Figures 2-17 and 2-18). Probability in this case means that the closer the slope steepness is to 39 degrees, the higher the probability of triggering an avalanche. Consequences mean that you visualize where an avalanche would take you and what would happen if you were swept into that location. The combination of the two determines the danger of the terrain.

To determine consequences, ask yourself, "What will happen if the slope slides?" Consequences can range from very safe to absolutely unsurvivable. Most people have an intuitive feel for how dangerous something is if they imagine themselves sliding down through the terrain at 60 mph. If it looks like it's dangerous, it probably is. Figure 2-16 shows four terrain examples with photos to illustrate their potential consequences.

Bad Consequences—What Will Happen If It Slides?

Terrain trap
(gully or sharp transition)

Trees (obstacles)

Cliffs, rocks, crevasses

Large slope

Figure 2-16. Here are four examples of terrain that is either un-survivable or has a low probability of a happy ending. In a terrain trap, even small avalanches can bury us too deeply to be dug out in time to save our life. Trees or rocks that we can hit on the way down are extremely dangerous. Slopes with rocks, cliffs, or crevasses are obviously nasty places. Large slopes not only have larger, more violent avalanches, but rescuers take longer to access the deposition zone, especially when coming from the top of the slope. In any of these situations, rescue has a low probability of success.

Notice that the danger of the terrain depends on the combination of steepness (probability) and consequences. Any time the slope steepness kicks up above about 30 degrees (including locally-connected terrain), I start paying lots of attention to consequences. If I don't like the consequences, then I have to either seek other terrain or make very sure the snowpack is very stable (as we will learn in the following chapters). Terrain around 39 degrees with safe consequences (such as a 3-meter-high road cut) are what I call test slopes because you can safely jump on them to see how the snowpack responds. Take some time to work through the

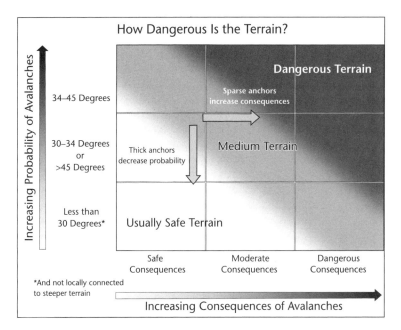

Figure 2-17. This is a simplified way I like to teach the danger of avalanche terrain. Here, we use just the permanent, immovable terrain features of steepness, anchors, and consequences. Just imagine the terrain covered with a uniform, homogenous layer of snow, which does not vary by aspect or elevation. The danger of the terrain depends mostly on the balance between steepness and consequences. Anchors matter, too. With thick anchors, you can move the probability down one notch. But if the anchors are sparse, your best friend suddenly turns into your worst enemy, and anchors suddenly become giant baseball bats that can beat you up on the way down. Sparse anchors move the terrain at least one notch on the consequence scale.

examples on this and the following pages to judge the danger of the slope based on steepness, anchors, and consequences.

TAKE-HOME POINT

Good terrain skills primarily involve being a good judge of both steepness and consequences. It's essential for us to constantly evaluate both as we travel until those skills become completely intuitive.

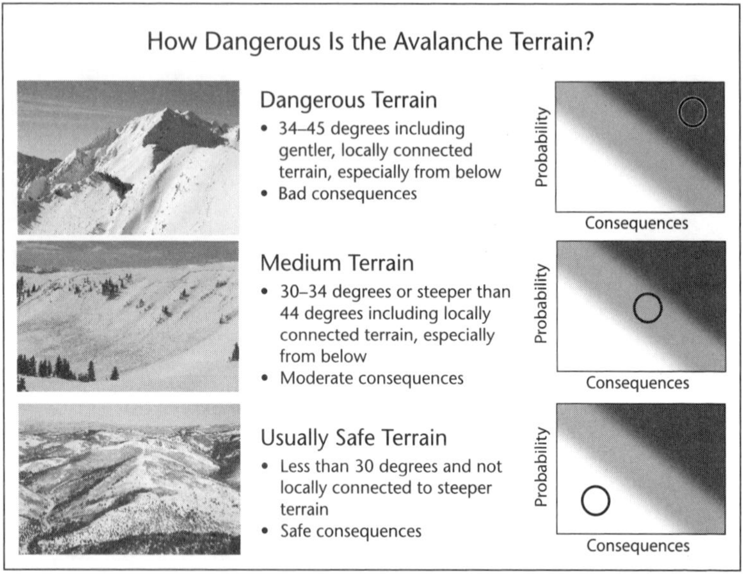
How Dangerous Is the Avalanche Terrain?
Dangerous Terrain
• 34–45 degrees including gentler, locally connected terrain, especially from below
• Bad consequences
Probability
Consequences
Medium Terrain
• 30–34 degrees or steeper than 44 degrees including locally connected terrain, especially from below
• Moderate consequences
Probability
Consequences
Usually Safe Terrain
• Less than 30 degrees and not locally connected to steeper terrain
• Safe consequences
Probability
Consequences

Figure 2-18. The danger of avalanche terrain is a combination of slope steepness, anchors, and consequences. We can display it as a probability-consequence diagram. Probability of avalanching is determined by steepness and anchors. Consequences are determined by terrain traps such as trees, cliffs, rocks, a large avalanche path, or sharp transitions to flatter slope angles. (Medium terrain photo courtesy USFS, Craig Gordon)

Safer Consequences

Safer consequences mean that if you were caught in an avalanche on that slope, it would probably result in no injury or only minor injuries—assuming you are with a partner and have all the proper rescue gear (see Chapter 8). Examples of safer consequences range from a small test slope to a small slope less than 15 vertical meters (50 feet) with no obstacles or terrain traps, a gentle transition, and a fan-shaped run out (where debris would spread out instead of concentrate). (Figures 2-19, 2-20, and 2-21.) Remember, it's not just about the size of the slope, it's what will happen to you if it slides. A small slope that terminates in a terrain trap, such as a narrow gully, is a very dangerous slope because even a small avalanche can bury you very deeply. Yes, we can definitely die on slopes with "safer consequences," so remember this is a relative term.

Figure 2-19. The slope in the foreground is steep with no anchors (high probability) but has relatively safer consequences since it is relatively small with no obstacles. I often use this as a test slope before I go into the much more dangerous terrain above. As always, my partner waits in a safe location in case something goes wrong. Notice that the wind is blowing hard on the slopes above, rapidly loading them with drifted snow, but it is not blowing nearly as hard on the smaller test slope. So on a day like this, the smaller slope is not representative of wind slab hazard.

Figure 2-20. This is an example of high probability and low consequences, because it is a small avalanche path and you can nip at the edges of the steep section. You could use the even smaller rollovers in the area as a test slope.

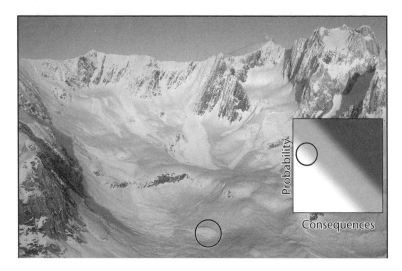

Figure 2-21. A small slope with low consequences would make a good test slope.

Medium Consequences

On a slope with medium consequences, you face possible injury or death should it avalanche (Figures 2-22 and 2-23). An example would be a medium-size slope of 15 to 90 vertical meters (50 to 300 vertical feet) with a gentle transition at the bottom.

Bad Consequences

A slope with bad consequences is one that will lead to almost certain injury or death. Some examples of terrain with bad consequences include these:

- ❖ A slope of any size that terminates in a terrain trap, a bench, trees, brush, a large cliff (Figure 2-24), an icefall, or crevasses. Remember that gullies are not half-pipes; they are terrain traps that can kill in the wrong conditions.
- ❖ Funnel-shaped avalanche paths, because even small avalanches will bury a victim very deeply in this terrain.
- ❖ Large avalanche paths (Figure 2-25). It's difficult to survive something like a 700-vertical-meter (2300-foot-long) ride in an avalanche, both because of the inherent trauma of a large avalanche and because it takes your partner a long time to access the debris to dig you out.
- ❖ Avalanche paths through sparse or thinly spaced trees, where the trees serve as false anchors (Figure 2-26).

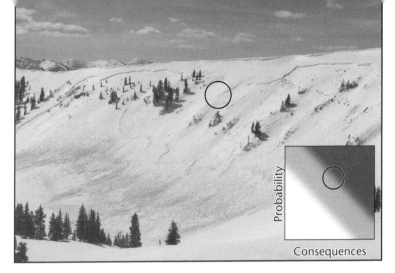

Figure 2-22. This slope has medium consequences since there are few trees to hit and it has a gentle transition.

Figure 2-23. This slope has medium consequences since it has a clean run out with few obstacles, so you at least have a chance to survive the ride. Notice that the prominent gully in the center of the photo has a high probability (because of steepness and being recently wind loaded), and it also has a high consequence because the debris concentrates in a terrain trap, making for a deep burial.

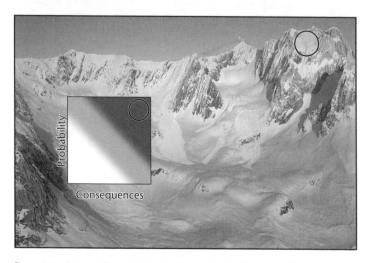

Figure 2-24 . A slope with very high probability combined with unsurvivable consequences, so it's a zero-tolerance-for-error slope. Obviously this is a slope we can cross only during very stable conditions. At least the consequences are very clear.

Figure 2-25. This terrain is very deceptive because from the top it seems much safer than it is. This small opening at the top is relatively gentle but if you trigger an avalanche, you will be strained through a line of trees and and pinball down a long, steep glade of trees. It would be almost impossible to survive an avalanche in this terrain.

Figure 2-26. This is much more dangerous than it seems because you would be strained through the many trees and deposited into a sharp, deep terrain trap at the bottom. An avalanche here would be almost impossible to survive.

TAKE-HOME POINT

Slopes with unsurvivable consequences have a zero tolerance for error. Always avoid them except in extremely stable conditions. They are like base jumping—one mistake and you're done.

ASPECT—WIND

Now that we have developed our eyes for spotting steepness, anchors, and consequences, we can start adding some of the snowpack variables—how the slope is affected by wind and how the resulting snowpack varies with terrain.

A slope's aspect—the direction it faces—with respect to the wind is a *huge* factor. This takes many people by surprise; human beings are big, heavy creatures, and most of the time, wind doesn't affect our lives very much. But imagine yourself as a bird—wind is your entire world. Then imagine yourself as something even

Photo 2-2. It's a sunny day but there is a blizzard going on. On this day, the wind was rapidly depositing snow onto downwind terrain, creating several large, natural avalanches that ran long distances.

smaller and lighter—like a feather or new fallen snow. Wind to a delicate snowflake is like the ocean current to plankton. Ignore it at your own peril.

Why is wind important? Weight added on top of buried weak layers (which we call "loading") causes most avalanches, and the fastest way to load a slope is with wind-drifted snow. Wind erodes snow from the upwind side of an obstacle, such as a ridge, to deposit it on the downwind side (Figure 2-27). We commonly see wind deposit snow 10 times more rapidly than snow falls from the sky during a storm (Photo 2-3).

Wind deposits snow most commonly on the leeward side of upper elevation prominent terrain features, such as ridges, peaks, and passes. We call this "top-loading." Wind can also blow across a slope, which we call "cross-loading," (Figure 2-28) and wind can even cause loading when it blows down a slope. Remember that wind can blow from any direction and thus deposit snow on almost any slope creating wind slabs.

Wind slabs are dangerous for the following reasons:

As the wind bounces eroded snow across the snow surface, it grinds up the snow into small, dense particles. When snow particles come to rest on the lee of

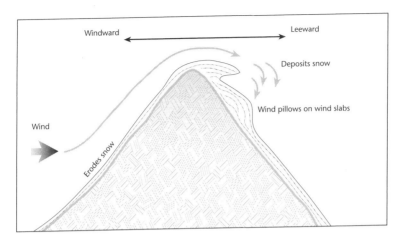

Figure 2-27. Typical wind-loading patterns

Photo 2-3. Wind can deposit snow 10 times more rapidly than can snow falling out of the sky. Wind erodes from the windward side and deposits on the lee side of any obstacle, such as a ridge. Wind-deposited snow can quickly overload buried weak layers.

Figure 2-28. Cross-loading and top-loading

an obstacle—where the wind slows down—they pack into a heavy, dense layer that not only can overload any buried weak layer but can create an overlying slab brittle enough to propagate cracks to larger areas.

When strong wind starts to blow, within minutes wind can turn nice fluffy powder into a dangerous wind slab. Safe conditions can quickly turn into dangerous conditions, which often take people by surprise.

Wind slabs can be highly localized. We often hear people say, "I was just walking along and suddenly the snow changed. It started cracking under my feet, and then the whole slope let loose."

TAKE-HOME POINT

Be suspicious of any steep slope with recent deposits of wind-drifted snow.

How to Recognize Wind Slabs

Luckily for us, wind creates easy-to-read textures on the snow surface, as well as characteristically shaped deposits. Thus, they are usually easy to recognize and avoid. No one should go into avalanche terrain without first learning how to read these obvious signs. An old avalanche hunter's adage: if you have developed a good eye for slope steepness and the effects of wind, you can avoid about 90 percent of all avalanches.

Wind slabs—also called pillows, deposited snow, or snow transport—are smooth and rounded, lens- or pillow-shaped, and a chalky white color (Figure 2-29). A wind

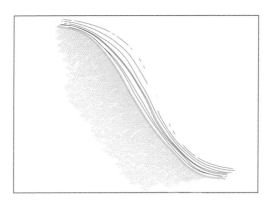

Figure 2-29. The smooth, rounded "pillow" of a wind slab

slab feels "slabby" (i.e., like harder snow on top of softer snow). It often sounds hollow like a drum—the more drumlike, the more dangerous. Often you'll notice the following:

- ❖ Cracks shoot away from you—the longer the crack, the more dangerous.
- ❖ A harder surface layer with softer snow below—you can easily feel this with a ski pole, by digging down with your hand, or as a snowmobile track punching through.
- ❖ Trail breaking can be difficult—you keep falling through the slab.
- ❖ It can range from very soft to so hard that you can hardly kick a boot into it.

A wind slab means that weight has been added to the snowpack. If the weight has been added recently and it's on a steep slope without anchors, then it almost always means danger. When you find a wind slab on a steep slope, you should:

- ❖ Stop immediately! Don't go any farther!
- ❖ Back off to a safe spot and dig down to investigate how well the slab is bonded to the underlying snow (see Chapter 3).
- ❖ Jump on a few safe test slopes to see how the snow responds.

If the slab breaks away easily on your tests, don't cross larger slopes. Go back the way you came or find another route that avoids wind slabs or uses slopes of less than 30 degrees.

If you absolutely have to cross the slope (and I can think of few reasons why you have to cross a dangerous slope without delving into B-movie plot devices), stay on the extreme upper edge of the wind slab, wear a belay rope tied to a solid anchor, and hope the crown fracture breaks at your feet instead of above you. Hard slabs tend to break above you, leaving you on the wrong side of the fracture line; soft, shallow slabs tend to break at your feet, leaving you on the good side of the fracture line. Realize, however, that "manageable" soft slabs can quickly turn into "unmanageable" hard slabs—sometimes just within a few feet.

ASPECT—SUN

The direction a slope faces (aspect) with respect to the sun also has a profound influence on the snowpack. Usually you need years of experience to appreciate the importance of aspect regarding the sun. You might not know your north, south, east, and west—but you had better learn, because people who don't know the aspect of the slope they are standing on have missed one of the most important pieces of the avalanche puzzle. To determine direction, use a compass, watch, or smartphone. Use your compass often, and work on developing a constant awareness for slope aspect.

The influence of aspect with respect to the sun is most important at midlatitudes, say, from about 30 degrees north latitude to around 55 degrees north latitude—in the Northern Hemisphere, from about the southern US border to about the northern British Columbia border. At equatorial latitudes, the sun is almost straight overhead, shining fairly equally on all slopes. At arctic latitudes,

Figure 2-30. The importance of aspect varies with latitude. In the continental United States, aspect is very important but is increasingly less important as you travel north or south.

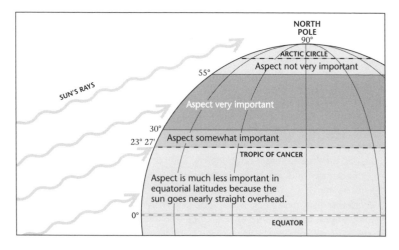

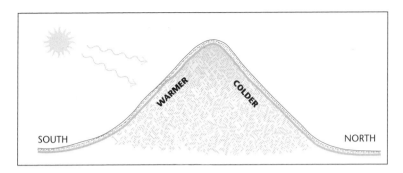

Figure 2-31. East-facing slopes are colder than west-facing slopes.

in the winter, the sun is too low on the horizon to provide much heat; but in fall and spring, aspects are more important. (See Figure 2-30). Remember that in the Southern Hemisphere the situation with respect to season is just the opposite.

Cold Snowpack

A cold snowpack tends to develop persistent weak layers more than a warm snowpack does, and weak layers persist longer. A cold snowpack commonly develops notoriously fragile weak layers, such as faceted snow and surface hoar. Largely because of this, the lion's share of avalanche accidents occur on north- and east-facing slopes, partly because that is where we find the best snow and consequently people tend to trigger more avalanches there, but mostly because those slopes exhibit more persistent weak layers.

North-facing slopes receive very little heat from the sun in midwinter. Conversely, south-facing slopes receive much more heat. Therefore, a north-facing slope will usually develop a dramatically different snowpack than a south-facing slope.

East-facing slopes catch sun only in the morning when temperatures are colder; west-facing slopes catch the sun in the warm afternoon. Consequently, east-facing slopes are colder than west-facing slopes (Figure 2-31).

In wet snow conditions due to strong sun, it's just the opposite of a dry snow-pack: South- and west-facing slopes usually produce more wet avalanches than the shadier slopes—at least at the beginning of a wet slide avalanche cycle in spring. In those conditions, the north-facing slopes are usually less dangerous.

During prolonged cloudy or stormy conditions when the sun seldom shines on the snow, little difference exists between sunny and shady slopes.

TAKE-HOME POINT

Seemingly subtle differences in the direction a slope faces with respect to the sun can have a huge effect on the stability of the snow. I can't count the number of accidents I have investigated in which people started riding in a bowl on a safe aspect, but as they used up the snow, they not only gained confidence but also tended to slowly work their way around the bowl onto the progressively more dangerous aspects, until someone finally triggered an avalanche.

ALTITUDE

In general, you will find more avalanche activity the higher you go on a mountain. Why? More wind, more snow, more cold, fewer anchors, more variability in the snowpack, and steeper terrain. Terrain above tree line is almost always more dangerous. In general, you should travel in alpine terrain only during stable conditions. When ascending, I always get suspicious when I'm crossing that final 100 meters (300 vertical feet) below a ridgeline or summit because more wind blows near ridges.

On the other hand, in some cases it's more dangerous at lower altitudes. Two common examples are (1) during wet avalanche conditions such as a rapid thaw of recently cold, dry snow or when rain falls at lower elevations; or (2) when surface hoar (frost) commonly forms at lower elevations where cooler, more saturated air pools. When we add a slab on top of a surface hoar layer, it's almost always dangerous because of the weak layer that forms.

COMPLEXITY

Canadian avalanche forecaster and guide Grant Statham came up with a wonderful checklist to rate the danger of the terrain on a larger scale, and this basic terrain classification has proved very useful in planning for an outing in a general area. (For traveling in specific terrain, use standard field skills discussed above in this chapter.) The Canadians rate most of their popular tours using this system, and they assign each tour with a three-step rating:

   ❖ Simple (see Photo 2-4)
   ❖ Challenging (see Photo 2-5)
   ❖ Complex (see Photos 2-6 and 2-7)

This rating system has proved to be quite popular, and Canadians have already mapped much of their terrain. You will likely see this basic terrain classification used more and more in the United States. It reflects not only the amount of avalanche terrain but how committing it is. See Table 2-2.

Photo 2-4. Simple Terrain—mostly low-angle or forested terrain with many terrain choices—is a good place to recreate in red-light avalanche conditions.

Photo 2-5. Challenging Terrain—well-defined avalanche paths with options to reduce exposure. If you know what you are doing, you can recreate here in yellow- or red-light avalanche conditions (stay in densely spaced trees and lower angled terrain).

Photo 2-6. Complex Terrain—multiple, overlapping avalanche paths and large expanses of open terrain with minimal options to reduce exposure. You can go here only during green-light avalanche conditions.

Photo 2-7. This complex terrain is the kind of place you go only when conditions are very stable. Most of it has zero tolerance for error because of bad consequences (cliffs, rocks, and terrain traps).

TABLE 2-2. TERRAIN COMPLEXITY CLASSIFICATION	
Terrain Rating	Summary of Characteristics
Simple	Exposure to low-angle or primarily forested terrain. Some forest openings may involve the run-out zones of infrequent avalanches. Many options to reduce or eliminate exposure. No glacier travel.
Challenging	Exposure to well-defined avalanche paths, starting zones, or terrain traps; options exist to reduce or eliminate exposure with careful routefinding. Glacier travel is straightforward but crevasse hazards may exist.
Complex	Exposure to multiple, overlapping avalanche paths or large expanses of steep, open terrain; multiple avalanche starting zones and terrain traps below; minimal options to reduce exposure. Complicated glacier travel with extensive crevasse bands or icefalls.

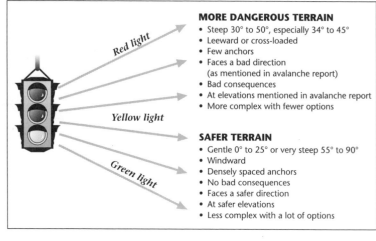

MORE DANGEROUS TERRAIN
- Steep 30° to 50°, especially 34° to 45°
- Leeward or cross-loaded
- Few anchors
- Faces a bad direction
  (as mentioned in avalanche report)
- Bad consequences
- At elevations mentioned in avalanche report
- More complex with fewer options

SAFER TERRAIN
- Gentle 0° to 25° or very steep 55° to 90°
- Windward
- Densely spaced anchors
- No bad consequences
- Faces a safer direction
- At safer elevations
- Less complex with a lot of options

Figure 2-32. The trusty "Tremper Terrain-o-Meter" illustrates the spectrum of terrain between very safe and very dangerous.

For instance, on a day of high or extreme avalanche danger, the worst place to plan for an outing is in "complex" terrain, which has large avalanche paths, overlapping run outs, many terrain traps, and few options to avoid danger (see Photo 2-7). Figure 2-32 lists red-yellow-green lights when judging the safety of dangerous terrain. It is a summary checklist of all the factors we consider when looking at terrain, including both strictly terrain features as well as how the snowpack varies with terrain. Terrain can range from being very dangerous to very safe with an infinite range and combinations between the factors. Terrain is like the steering wheel in our car; our choice of terrain is the main way we control our own risk. When the snowpack is dangerous, we steer towards safer terrain. When the snowpack is very safe, we have the choice to head to more dangerous terrain. Thus, learning to read avalanche terrain is an essential skill and one that often takes several years to master.

CHAPTER 3

HOW DANGEROUS
IS THE SNOWPACK?

Snow is often like one of those difficult lovers we have all pursued at some point in our lives—the ones our parents and friends warned us about: complex, change-able over both time and space, fickle, guilty-until-proven-innocent, the source of both ecstasy and tragedy. Yet snow can also be a reliable, steady partner you want to bring home to meet the parents and build your life around. Learning the differ-ence between the two is an essential skill both in matters of love and matters of avalanches. This chapter takes a closer look at the snowpack.

HOW AVALANCHES WORK

Let's start with some avalanche basics. Yes, avalanches also occur as loose snow avalanches, or "sluffs" as we call them, but slab avalanches account for the vast majority of avalanche deaths in North America. Thus, not surprisingly, 90 percent of this book focuses on how to avoid getting caught in slab avalanches.

Picture a magazine held by friction on an inclined table. Then imagine you're standing on the middle of that magazine, as it overcomes friction to start sliding off the table. You are moving with it, the edges are distant, and suddenly there's no escape. In the backcountry, the magazine represents a snow slab rocketing downhill with you as its unintended passenger—off for the most terrifying and dangerous ride of your life.

If you look at avalanche accidents in the United States, a typical slab is 60 centime-ters deep and 60 meters wide (about 2 feet deep and about two-thirds the size of a football field wide). It usually reaches speeds of 30 km per hour (20 mph) within the first three seconds and quickly accelerates to around 130 km per hour (80 mph) after the first, say, six seconds. The bonds holding a slab in place fracture at about 350 km

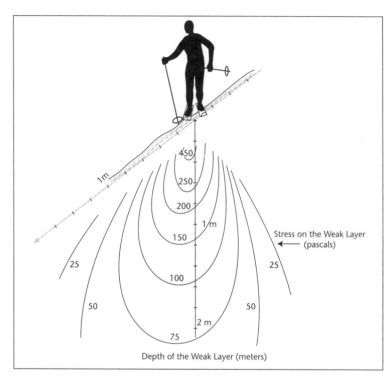

Figure 3-1. Additional stress the snow feels when you cross it. The units are pascals. Notice that the deeper a weak layer is buried, the less additional stress a person will exert on it. (From the Swiss Institute of Snow and Avalanche Research)

per hour (220 mph), and the slab appears to shatter like glass. As it continues down it breaks up further, forming a furious and fast-moving mass of cascading snow.

Dry slab avalanches can lie teetering on the verge of catastrophe, sometimes for several days. The weak layers beneath slabs are extremely sensitive to the rate at which they are stressed. And, just like people, the snowpack does not like rapid change, which can make an otherwise benign snowpack very cranky. Then, the mere weight of a person can easily push it over the edge (Figure 3-1). If you are on a snowmobile, realize that a snowmobile with a person onboard exerts 2.5–5 times the amount of stress on buried weak layers than a person alone. Like a giant booby trap, avalanches can lie in waiting for just the right person to come along. The fracture

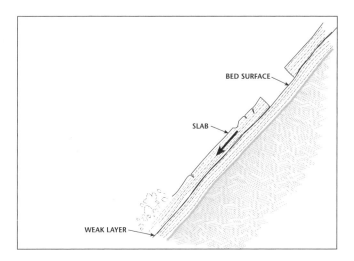

Figure 3-2. Parts of a slab avalanche

line often forms well above the victim, leaving little room for escape. This sounds dangerous because it is.

Parts of a Slab Avalanche

A slab avalanche has three components (Figure 3-2):

- ❖ Slab: Relatively harder or more cohesive snow that slides
- ❖ Weak layer or weak interface: Relatively weaker or less cohesive snow that fractures, causing the slab to slide
- ❖ Bed surface: Harder layer of snow that the slab slides upon; the ground can also be a bed surface (a preexisting bed surface is not required— often the avalanche creates its own bed surface)

What Makes a Slab?

Weather deposits snow in layers. Each different kind of weather affects the snow in a different way: Sunshine makes a sun crust. Wind erodes snow from the upwind side of a ridge and deposits that same snow on the downwind side in a dense wind slab (see Aspect—Wind in Chapter 2). Clear skies at night create a layer of frost (surface hoar) on the surface of the snow. And so on.

As each storm buries the layers, the snowpack becomes a complex stack of layers, some relatively stronger and some relatively weaker. When stronger snow overlies weaker snow, we call it a slab. Or as Karl Birkeland of the Forest Service National Avalanche Center puts it, "A slab is when you have something sitting on top of nothing."

Remember that a slab doesn't have to be so hard that you can hardly kick your boot into it. It just has to be *relatively* stronger than the snow underneath. Light, dry powder snow can behave as a slab as long as it has an even weaker layer underneath.

What Makes a Weak Layer?

Nearly any kind of snow can be a weak layer or a weak interface, but weak layers tend to be these, listed roughly in order of importance:

- ❖ Faceted snow—very weak, angular, larger-grained snow that forms within the snowpack because of large temperature gradients within the snowpack
- ❖ Surface hoar—a fancy name for frost that forms on the snow surface and, when buried, creates a particularly dangerous weak layer
- ❖ Low-density or poorly bonded layers within new snow—such as stellar crystals or plates (like a snowflake design on a sweater) or graupel (pellet snow like tiny Styrofoam balls, which can behave like little ball bearings)
- ❖ A weak interface—such as new snow sliding on a slippery ice crust

In this book, I do not explain the details of how various weak layers form. If you're interested, read my book *Staying Alive in Avalanche Terrain,* which goes into much more detail on everything discussed in this book, including the physical properties and formation of snow crystals and layers.

What Makes a Bed Surface?

A bed surface is a layer of relatively harder snow (or ground) on which the slab slides. You don't need a preexisting bed surface to make an avalanche. For instance, sometimes avalanches fracture within a thick layer of weak snow, and the avalanche creates its own bed surface as the avalanche descends. But in most cases, avalanches descend on a harder, slicker snow surface in the same way that a magazine (the slab) slides off the surface of an inclined table (the bed surface). Common bed surfaces include the following:

- ❖ Rain crusts
- ❖ Sun crusts
- ❖ Hard, old snow surface
- ❖ Wind-hardened snow (see Aspect—Wind in Chapter 2)
- ❖ Melt-freeze crusts

Figure 3-3. Strong snowpacks can support large amounts of stress, but weak snowpacks are easily overloaded by the same stress. (From *Snow Sense*, Jill Fredston and Doug Fesler)

Recipe for a Slab Avalanche

To cook up a slab avalanche, you need to gather up the following ingredients:

❖ A slope steep enough to slide—a slope generally steeper than about 30 degrees (34–45 degrees is best)

❖ A weak layer

❖ A slab on top of the weak layer

❖ A trigger

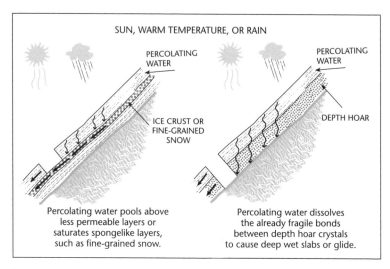

Figure 3-4. Two common examples of wet slab avalanches

Finally, you need the secret ingredient: rapid change. If you remember nothing else from this chapter, remember that, just like people, snow does not like rapid change. (Raise gas prices slowly enough and no one even notices; raise them two dollars overnight and you will have riots at the gas pump.) Likewise, buried weak layers are very sensitive to the rate at which they are stressed. Like people, they get cranky. Rapid changes that affect snowpack operate on a time scale from about an hour to a day. For the vast majority of slab avalanches, this means the addition of weight from either windblown snow or new snow. In rarer cases, it means the rapid warming of the overlying slab.

We can think of it as strength versus stress. I like to use Jill Fredston and Doug Fesler's example of a weight lifter (strength) holding up weight (stress). We need to know both sides of the equation—the strength of the weight lifter as well as the amount of weight he attempts to hold up. Notice in Figure 3-3 that we can make the weight lifter's knees shaky either by adding more weight or by decreasing his strength (tickling him).

Not all buried weak layers are the same; some are stronger than others. With a strong buried weak layer, you may be able to add waist-deep new snow without any problem, but with a fragile weak layer, perhaps only ankle-deep snow will push it over the edge. Remember, we're talking about the *weight* of the snow, not its depth. Ankle-deep, heavy, wet snow can weigh just as much as waist-deep powder.

It gets even trickier when we talk about rapid change due to rapidly rising temperature. In this case, temperature changes the properties of the snow without adding any weight (tickling the weight lifter). Snow is always moving slowly downhill (called "creep"), although it occurs so slowly we can't see it. Rapidly rising temperature or the onset of rain can increase the creep rate of the slab, which causes increased stress on a buried weak layer, plus the slab becomes more flexible so the weight of people can more easily initiate a fracture in the layers below.

Also, with prolonged melting of a recently cold, dry snowpack, meltwater percolates through the snowpack, which comes as quite a shock to buried, cold, dry weak layers (Figure 3-4). To get a feel for how a snowpack feels with a rapid temperature change, jump into a cold shower.

Figure 3-5. When a person or snowmobile triggers an avalanche, the initial fracture occurs within the weak layer under or near the person because their weight exerts too much additional stress on the buried weak layer. The fracture then spreads outward through the weak layer. Finally, after the slab has detached on the bottom, gravity pulls the slab downhill creating visible fracture lines in the snow on the surface, which although they are the most visible to us, are actually the last fractures to occur. (From "Avalanche Release," a presentation by Ian McCammon)

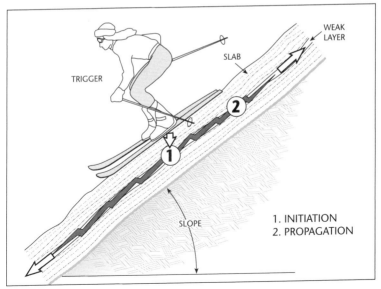

WEAK LAYER

SLAB

TRIGGER

SLOPE

1. INITIATION
2. PROPAGATION

Triggering a Slab Avalanche

Now for the final ingredient: the trigger. A slab avalanche occurs when the weak layer collapses in a localized area and that collapse continues to spread outward in all directions (propagates). Once the collapse breaks all the crystalline bonds between the slab and the bed surface, the slab is free to start sliding down the slope, provided it can overcome friction and the pinning effect of anchors such as trees. This all occurs very fast; it looks like a shattering pane of glass.

In 93 percent of avalanche accidents, humans trigger the avalanche. When rapid change makes the snowpack cranky, just the additional weight of a person or a snowmobile can trigger the avalanche (Figure 3-5). And if that trigger—that would be you or me—finds him or herself on the wrong side of the fracture line, in an instant we become an unintended passenger on many tons of moving snow, which quickly accelerates to freeway speed, putting us at the mercy of unspeakable power and violence—wherever its physics take us.

Shear Quality

Avalanche professionals pay close attention to what we call "shear quality"—and you should too. Fractures can occur on layers ranging from very thin to very thick. Although all these layers fail in compression, some layers are so thin that they seem to pop out instead of collapse. What we call a Quality 1 shear is a smooth fracture along a single plane that either pops out with a lot of energy, like a cash register drawer, or fails in a sudden collapse—"pops and drops" as the Canadians call them. This means danger.

TRAVEL ADVICE FOR DIFFERENT TYPES OF AVALANCHES

In the movie *How to Train Your Dragon*, all the potential young dragon hunters go to a school where they spend most of their time learning about different kinds of dragons and the techniques that work best to vanquish each kind. This is exactly how avalanche professionals teach students about avalanches. As my mentor, Doug Fesler, taught me so many years ago, "First you have to know what kind of avalanche dragon you're dealing with."

Typically, two to three different kinds of avalanches exist on the same mountain on the same day. For instance, you may find wind slabs up high along the ridges, persistent slabs on north- through east-facing slopes, and wet avalanches at low elevations. The avalanche advisory will often contain graphics and a discussion on each type of problem. Each avalanche dragon differs by where we find them, how we recognize them, how we travel through terrain, and how dangerous they are. This section provides a quick overview. We will start with the easier dragons and progress to the trickier, more deadly ones.

Photo 3-1. A skier triggering a small loose snow avalanche, also called a "sluff." © Scott Markewitz

Loose Dry Avalanches (aka Sluffs)

Sluffs are simply loose, new-snow avalanches—not slabs. These avalanches usually start at a point and fan outward as they descend. They typically occur on steep slopes (over 40 degrees) during or just after a storm. They commonly stabilize quickly, within hours or a day after the storm. These are often referred to as "harmless sluffs," which they usually are, unless one carries you into a terrain trap or over a cliff. Also, some small sluffs can build into quite large masses of snow, especially if they descend in big terrain. See Photo 3-1.

Travel Advice

Avoid terrain traps or large, steep slopes until they have stabilized. You can use slope cuts (see Snowpack Tests in Chapter 4) on dry sluffs. If you descend in sluffing conditions, travel across or diagonally to the fall line to avoid being caught in sluffs you trigger.

Loose Wet Avalanches

Loose wet avalanches are similar to loose dry avalanches, but they occur when the surface snow becomes wet and thus loses strength from strong sun, warm temperatures, or rain. These avalanches are more powerful and dangerous than dry sluffs because they are denser and pack more of a punch. Pinwheels or rollerballs of snow often occur when cold, dry snow becomes wet for the first time. They often precede wet sluffs. See Photo 3-2.

Travel Advice

Avoid steep slopes or passing beneath them when loose wet avalanches are active. You don't want to get caught in one of these. With lots of experience, you can use slope cuts on them, but don't underestimate them.

Wet Slab Avalanches

Wet slab avalanches occur when percolating water from melting snow or rain decreases the strength of a buried weak layer. These can be very large, destructive, and deadly avalanches. See Photo 3-3. Luckily, not many avalanche deaths occur from wet slabs because they are more difficult for people to trigger than dry slab avalanches, so they tend to occur naturally during strong melting or during intense rain. Also, people tend to avoid wet snow conditions.

Travel Advice

Avoid them. Stay off and out from underneath avalanche terrain during strong melting by sun or warm temperatures or during rain. Warning: Most stability tests don't work well on wet slabs, and neither do slope cuts.

Photo 3-2. Warm, sunny conditions have created wet avalanche conditions. We can see that a previous skier triggered a small, wet sluff. The best sign of avalanches are avalanches, so this might not be the smartest time to ascend an adjacent slope.

Cornice Breaks

Cornices are beautiful, overhanging, cantilevered snow structures along ridges where the wind has deposited them on the downwind side. Hazard from cornices can linger long after a storm, but it's especially easy to trigger a cornice break during or just after a storm or during very warm temperatures. I've had three very close calls when I've unintentionally triggered a cornice break. Treat cornices with a large dose of extra caution. They often break farther back than you'd expect, and the weight of a falling cornice often triggers a larger, deeper avalanche when it hits the slope below. See Photo 3-4.

Travel Advice

Avoid them. Never walk up to the edge of a drop-off in the mountains without wearing a rope or first getting a good look at it out from a safe spot. You can use smaller cornices as a stability test if you know what you are doing (see Snowpack Tests in Chapter 4).

Photo 3-3. Avalanche control with explosives and heavy ski compaction are very effective at preventing large slab avalanches at ski resorts. However, especially with depth hoar near the ground, when the entire snowpack becomes saturated for the first time, it's possible for large, wet slabs to fracture, taking out the entire season's snowpack, complete with moguls. This was an explosive-triggered avalanche at a resort around noon on a very hot spring day.

Photo 3-4. Never walk up to a drop-off without first checking it out from another vantage point or wearing a rope. Most of the time, you will be standing on nothing but air. Cornices are extremely dangerous.

Storm Slab Avalanches

Storm slabs are simply avalanches within new snow, and they are relatively easy to detect. These are usually soft slabs caused by differences in density, moisture, or crystal types of the falling snow. For instance, if storm snow starts out warmer and wetter and finishes drier and lighter, it's what we call "right side up" snow—just the way we like it: heavy on the bottom, light on top. But sometimes the storm does the opposite, laying down heavier, denser snow on top of lighter, fluffier snow, which creates "upside down" snow, which can slide as a soft slab. See Photo 3-5. The good news is that storm snow usually "settles out" (stabilizes) rather quickly— usually within a few hours to a day.

Travel Advice

Storm slabs are easy to see and feel because they are right on the surface. You can easily dig down with your hand and pull on little blocks to see how the snow behaves or, better yet, jump on small test slopes to see how they respond. Shallow, soft slabs usually respond well to slope cuts and test slopes but, as usual, avoid slope cuts on deeper or harder slabs. Do quick "hand pit tests" as you travel to test how well the snow is bonded (see Snowpack Tests in Chapter 4).

Photo 3-5. A common pattern with storm slab avalanches. Here we see many smaller avalanches occurring during or immediately after a storm. As the slab gains strength, avalanches become harder to trigger, but fractures propagate farther and create larger, more dangerous avalanches. © Jürg Schweizer

Figure 3-6. It's extremely important to develop your avalanche eyeballs to see the difference between wind-eroded snow and wind-deposited snow. Here, wind has cross-loaded gullies in the early season and the wind slabs have overloaded fragile depth hoar. Eroded snow (usually safe) has a rough, sandblasted look while wind-deposited snow (usually dangerous) is smooth and rounded. Often just a few inches separate very safe snow from very dangerous snow.

Wind Slab Avalanches

Wind slab avalanches are a common avalanche triggered by people, so it's essential to learn to recognize and avoid them. Wind slabs form when wind erodes snow from the upwind side of an obstacle like a ridge and deposits snow on the downwind side (see Figure 3-6). You find them especially near ridges, but they are often cross-loaded onto the sides of gullies; complex wind patterns can form complex wind deposits.

Like storm snow, wind slabs can be easy to detect because they are right on the surface and you can usually recognize them by their smooth, rounded shape as opposed to the sandblasted look of eroded snow. They also often sound hollow like a drum or feel "slabby"—strong snow with weaker snow underneath.

Caveat: When fresh wind slabs are covered by recent snow without wind, they become invisible, hidden beneath the perfect façade.

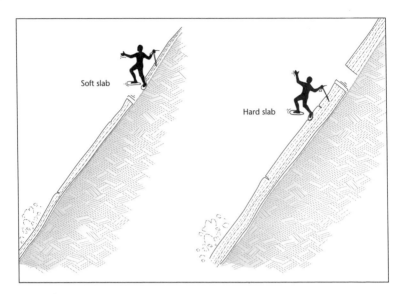

Figure 3-7. Soft, shallow slabs tend to break at your feet. Hard or thick slabs tend to break above you.

The tricky thing about wind slabs is that they can range from being very soft to very hard and also from being very shallow to very deep.

Travel Advice

Soft, shallow wind slabs are safer because they tend to break at your feet instead of above you and are easier to trigger, so you get a lot of instant feedback. With soft, shallow wind slabs, you can easily dig down with your hand and pull on small blocks to see how well they are bonded, and you can jump on small test slopes to see how they respond. But as the slab becomes harder or deeper, it is much more difficult to trigger (less feedback), and harder, deeper slabs tend to let you get farther out onto them before they break. The fracture forms up above you, and it's easy to find yourself on the wrong side of the fracture line. It's a fuzzy boundary between manageable wind slabs and unmanageable ones. Thus, even the pros get fooled occasionally and find themselves on the wrong side of the fracture line (Figure 3-7).

For experienced and skilled folks, test slopes and slope cuts work for shallow, soft wind slabs but are quite dangerous for deep or hard wind slabs. It takes a lot of experience to know the difference. So if you don't have much experience with wind slabs, just avoid them. The best place to gain experience is on small test slopes with safe consequences, such as a road cut or a small slope, say less than 6 meters (20 feet) high (see Snowpack Tests in Chapter 4).

Persistent Slab Avalanches

Yikes! These are the dangerous ones—to be avoided at all costs. In Switzerland and Canada, 82 percent of avalanche fatalities occur when the victim triggers a persistent slab. We call them "persistent" because the culprit weak layer continues to produce avalanches for several days—sometimes a week or more—after a storm. Plus, they can be dormant for a while before being reactivated by storms, which makes them especially tricky. Persistent slabs have to be matched by equally persistent patience. See Photo 3-6.

Persistent weak layers usually form during clear weather. These weak layers don't fall from the sky; they form in place within the snowpack. They are composed of either (1) faceted snow (sparkly large-grained snow) caused by large temperature gradients within the snowpack, or (2) sparkly surface hoar (frost) deposited on the snow surface then buried by subsequent storms.

Persistent slabs are especially tricky and deadly for the following reasons:

❖ They can vary in size from shallow to deep.

❖ With surface hoar as the weak layer, avalanches can run on surprisingly gentle slopes—sometimes on slopes of 30 degrees or less.

❖ Persistent slabs are often localized to specific terrain—usually sheltered, shady slopes without wind. So, counter intuitively, you may not find them near ridges, where storm snow and wind slabs usually hang out, but instead in sheltered, shady slopes, which means you can trigger lingering persistent slabs in places you normally don't see avalanches.

❖ They often produce "alarm signals" (sounds of collapsing or cracking) after they are buried by the first storm but may not produce alarm signals when subsequent storms reactivate them.

❖ They often have no visible clues from the surface, so the only way you can detect persistent slabs is by digging a lot of snow pits.

❖ They tend to fracture above you instead of at your feet.

❖ They are often triggered remotely from locally connected terrain, which is especially bad news when triggered from the bottom.

❖ They can break wide and large, crossing terrain features and breaking into adjacent slide paths.

❖ They often have lingering pockets of instability that persist long after other areas and other types of avalanches have stabilized.

Photo 3-6. Average-size slab avalanche caused by a persistent weak layer. Dry slab avalanches range from very hard to very soft. Soft slabs are composed of mostly new snow, while hard slabs are composed of either old, harder layers of snow or wind slabs.)
© Karl Birkeland

Travel Advice

Persistent slabs are your basic nightmare. You can manage risk only by avoiding them or by making very conservative terrain choices (based on steepness and consequences). You have to give them plenty of extra time to stabilize after a storm—days or weeks versus one day—which goes against human nature. The cookie tastes best fresh out of the oven, but you need to be patient and wait a few days on this one. Most people don't. Thus, persistent slabs account for the vast majority of avalanche fatalities. When you dig in the snowpack, look for the big sparkly crystals with little strength. When they are cranky, they pop out with snow-pit tests like a spring-loaded cash register drawer or a sudden collapse (see Snowpack Tests in Chapter 4).

Deep, Persistent Slab Avalanches

If you think persistent slabs are dangerous, just wait until you encounter their big brother. Deep, persistent slabs are simply persistent slabs that have been buried

Photo 3-7. Here I am investigating a large, deep-slab avalanche. I love to examine avalanches that have just occurred because I can see the weak layer that produced the avalanche. Although it does not look like it, this is actually quite safe. I would rather be in this particular spot after the avalanche has occurred than before.

by several storms instead of just one or two. They exhibit all the properties listed above for persistent slabs, except they're harder to trigger—but if you do trigger one, it's huge. See Photo 3-7. They can easily break deeper than you are tall and wider than several football fields, propagating into several adjacent slide paths. Don't expect to survive one of these monsters.

Most of the time they are triggered from a place where the slab is shallow, such as near a windblown ridge or rock outcroppings on a slope or from the bottom. These are the bad boys that take out numerous previous tracks when someone tickles the right spot. In other words, low probability—high consequences. It's like playing Russian roulette with a pistol that has 99 empty chambers and 1 chamber loaded with a 44-magnum bullet.

Photo 3-8. It seems that this backcountry access gate at a Utah ski area would leave little doubt about the dangers of entering uncontrolled avalanche terrain, yet hundreds of people without any rescue gear or avalanche training parade through the gate every day.

Photo 3-9. A snowboarder was killed in a massive avalanche he triggered just past the ski area boundary, which had many previous tracks. It's hard to believe something is dangerous when every-one else is doing it, and it's hard to switch your thinking from the Disneyland safety of a ski area to the Stone Age savagery of the backcountry when merely crossing a thin, little rope line. Each year several people die exactly this way. To get a sense of the scale in this photo, note my cohorts examining the slide.

Travel Advice

Avoid them or make very conservative terrain choices. Most stability tests don't work, so don't be tempted to try to outsmart deep, persistent slabs; obvious clues like the Five Red Flags (see Chapter 4, Will It Slide?) don't work well either. Deep slabs fool many pros. And they break so deep and wide that even with the best rescue equipment in the world, you won't likely survive. Just don't mess with them.

HOW WEATHER AFFECTS THE SNOWPACK

Now that you are up to speed on how avalanches work and the different avalanche types, the next step is to see how the weather affects the snowpack, as well as how the weather influences the way you travel and where you can go.

Photo 3-10. It was a dark and stormy morning. Weather is the mother of all avalanches and when Momma ain't happy, ain't nobody happy.

Will the Weather Make the Snow More Stable or Less Stable?

Remember our mantra: Snow does not like rapid change. Rapid changes make the snowpack less stable; lack of rapid change makes the snowpack more stable.

Below are rapid weather changes, listed roughly in order of their importance:

❖ Recent deposits of wind-drifted snow—the deeper and denser the wind drifts, the more dangerous

❖ Recent new snow—the deeper and denser, the more dangerous

❖ Recent and rapid thaw of a cold, dry snowpack from sun, rain, or warm temperatures

❖ Recent and rapid temperature rise of a cold, dry snowpack—not the usual daytime warming but a significant, dramatic change such as when cold, dry weather suddenly changes to moist, warm weather

❖ Prolonged melting of a layered, winterlike snowpack—for instance, one to three days of strong melting without a strong overnight refreeze

If the forecast leads you to believe that any of the above will occur, then the snowpack will become less stable. If not, then the snowpack will likely become more stable.

TAKE-HOME POINT

Snow does not like rapid change. Boring weather creates boring avalanche conditions; exciting weather creates exciting avalanche conditions; unusual weather creates unusual avalanche conditions. Weather is the mother of avalanches, and when Momma ain't happy, ain't nobody happy.

CHAPTER 4

WILL IT SLIDE?

To answer the difficult question "Will it slide?" you don't have to go it alone. Start with the easy answers—advice from the pros and the wisdom of crowds—then progressively work your way into the harder questions, doing your own evaluation and stability tests. In this way, you also start with the big regional picture then work your way to the intermediate mountain-level scale, finally ending up on the local scale of a specific slope. This section looks first at advice from the pros, followed by evaluation and stability tests.

READ AVALANCHE ADVISORIES

Avalanche advisories are designed for people who have at least some sort of avalanche training, and they include many of the terms you would learn in an avalanche class: avalanche types, crystal types, terrain features. Advisories also provide another avenue to avalanche education: instant feedback. Read the advisory each morning and then go out to see what it was talking about and experience it for yourself.

A well-crafted avalanche advisory from an experienced forecaster is a thing of beauty. A team of avalanche professionals gather information from a variety of sources and condense it into an easily understandable summary of the critical information you need to stay alive in avalanche terrain. It's one of the best deals in town—and it's all free. It's an essential, daily newspaper for the backcountry.

Local avalanche advisories exist for many popular mountainous areas in the world. (See www.avalanche.org for a map linked to websites.) As you click around the United States, you will find a huge variation in the presentation, detail, and quality of the avalanche information from the various avalanche centers, corresponding to differences in funding, incoming data, and the size of the population served. Here I discuss the kinds of information you will typically find at the better-funded and more popular avalanche centers. The less information available from the local avalanche center, the more you have to become your own avalanche expert and do more of your own homework.

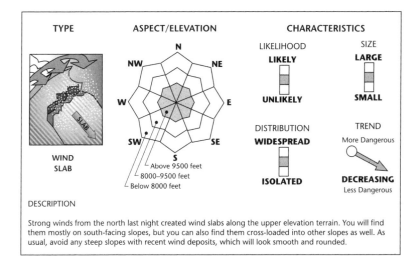

| TYPE | ASPECT/ELEVATION | CHARACTERISTICS |

TYPE

WIND
SLAB

ASPECT/ELEVATION

N
NW   NE
W   E
SW   SE
S
└ Above 9500 feet
└ 8000–9500 feet
└ Below 8000 feet

CHARACTERISTICS

LIKELIHOOD
LIKELY

UNLIKELY

DISTRIBUTION
WIDESPREAD

ISOLATED

SIZE
LARGE

SMALL

TREND
More Dangerous

DECREASING
Less Dangerous

DESCRIPTION

Strong winds from the north last night created wind slabs along the upper elevation terrain. You will find them mostly on south-facing slopes, but you can also find them cross-loaded into other slopes as well. As usual, avoid any steep slopes with recent wind deposits, which will look smooth and rounded.

Figure 4-1. Most avalanche advisories will tell you which kinds of avalanche problems you will encounter, and include graphics and a text description. According to this example, you will likely find wind slabs in the upper elevation, on wind-exposed terrain. Even though it states that wind came from the north overnight, wind swirls around a lot in the mountains, so you could find them on all the other aspects too. Bottom line: If you find a recent deposit of wind-drifted snow in avalanche terrain, avoid it.

Most avalanche centers offer several tiers of information ranging from basic regional-scale information to highly detailed information that can help users make slope-specific forecasts (Figure 4-1).

The Danger Rating: Regional Scale

For basic information for those who just want to know the general avalanche danger level, avalanche centers provide the overall danger rating on a five-step scale (Figure 4-2). This standardized international scale describes avalanche danger based on both probability and size. You often see the danger rating displayed as both an overall danger rating for a region as well as a way to describe more specific danger ratings by aspect and elevation.

Remember, these danger ratings are general and they apply only on a regional scale; thus, you can use them for regional (big-picture) decisions, but they are not intended for slope-scale (local) forecasts. For more detailed information, you must drill down deeper into the avalanche advisory and specific trip reports.

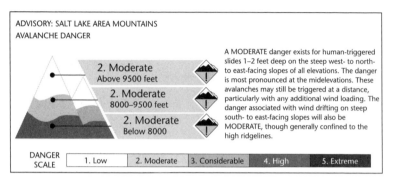

ADVISORY: SALT LAKE AREA MOUNTAINS
AVALANCHE DANGER

2. Moderate
Above 9500 feet

2. Moderate
8000–9500 feet

2. Moderate
Below 8000

A MODERATE danger exists for human-triggered slides 1–2 feet deep on the steep west- to north- to east-facing slopes of all elevations. The danger is most pronounced at the midelevations. These avalanches may still be triggered at a distance, particularly with any additional wind loading. The danger associated with wind drifting on steep south- to east-facing slopes will also be MODERATE, though generally confined to the high ridgelines.

DANGER SCALE	1. Low	2. Moderate	3. Considerable	4. High	5. Extreme

Figure 4-2. This is basic avalanche information with the overall danger rating by elevation band. This gives you the most basic information for pretrip planning purposes. But for mountain-scale (intermediate) or slope-scale (local) decisions, you need more detailed information from a full advisory, plus field skills learned in a multiday, field-based avalanche class.

Aspect and Altitude: Intermediate Scale

Avalanche hazard often varies dramatically by aspect and elevation (altitude), so most avalanche advisories provide some sort of graphic to help you visualize the pattern. Sometimes aspect and elevation are displayed in separate graphics, which is a bit easier for casual users to decipher. Some avalanche centers combine them both into one aspect-elevation diagram (also called a locator rose), which is a powerful graphic but one that takes some time to learn to use a locator. (Figure 4-1 includes a locator rose.)

Recent Avalanche Activity

The best sign of avalanches are…other avalanches. It's such an obvious clue that many people miss it. The thrust of this book is to systematically make evidence-based decisions, and there is no better evidence of avalanche danger than recent avalanche activity. If recent avalanches don't support your beliefs about avalanche danger, then it's time to update those beliefs or, better yet, learn to throw out a belief altogether. Thus, whenever avalanche professionals talk to each other, their first question is usually, "What kind of avalanche activity are you getting?" Most avalanche advisories will summarize recent avalanche activity.

Pay attention to the details in the advisory's text: location, aspect, elevation, depth, width, avalanche type, how far it is running, how it was triggered. It's a good idea to look at the advisory every day to stay abreast of the avalanche history. Otherwise, scroll back through the avalanche list from the previous few days to bring

Photo 4-1. Has this skier chosen a good route or a bad route? Hint: The avalanche occurred the day before. Actually, the skier's route is not nearly as dangerous as it looks because it's much more gentle than the slope that avalanched, and it faces east, whereas most of the slope that avalanched faces north. Still, if I just had to ski this slope, I would put my track right near the flank wall of the previous avalanche so that if the rest of the slope ripped out, at least I would have an escape route onto the bed surface of the previous avalanche.

yourself up to speed. Most avalanche centers also provide photos and videos of recent avalanche activity.

If your local avalanche center does not provide recent avalanche activity, then try to quiz local ski patrollers or guides.

Weather Forecasts

Luckily for us, we live in the Information Age, and a plethora of weather information and forecasts are just a click away. I have over 40 weather sites bookmarked, but then again, I'm an incorrigible weather weenie and it's part of my job. For most folks, just visiting the National Weather Service web page for your area is all you need. They offer automated, detailed weather forecasts for every 2.5-km (1.5 miles) grid point in the United States. How cool is that? Just set a point on your area of interest and bookmark it.

Terrain Maps

Yes, the Internet to our rescue once again! I can waste hours on Google Earth exploring terrain I'm unfamiliar with to help evaluate the terrain safety. I always set the elevation exaggeration to 1.0 for a more realistic view of the terrain steepness. Even on detailed paper maps you can measure steepness only to plus or minus 5 degrees, which is not nearly accurate enough for avalanche considerations. I'm afraid there's no substitute for measuring it on the ground.

The Canadians have mapped much of their terrain with respect to simple, challenging, and complex terrain, which you can view online at www.avalanche.ca. In the United States, where we have much less funding for anything spelled "avalanche," we just have to make do.

Make sure to also read competent guidebooks for the area you plan to visit.

MOUNTAIN-SCALE (INTERMEDIATE) EVALUATION

Now that you have the more generalized information from the avalanche advisory, it's time to start your mountain-scale (intermediate) evaluation: Basically, continue to observe as you make your approach to your chosen area.

Recent avalanches: I tend to be dangerous when I'm driving into the mountains because I'm always rubbernecking for avalanches. It's better to have the passenger look for avalanches. I keep binoculars in my car and use them often. I also travel in the field with a lightweight monocular, which doubles as a microscope for snow crystals. For me, it's an essential tool that I use for spotting fracture lines far more often than for looking at crystals. Look for those telltale horizontal lines in the snow, which are fracture lines at the crown face of the avalanche. Don't forget to look for small fractures on the road cuts as well as big fractures on the usual slopes.

Current weather: Observe current conditions carefully as you make your way to the slope. What speed and direction is the wind? What's the temperature? What's the sky doing—is it sunny, cloudy, raining? Is there fresh snow—what kind, how much?

Terrain complexity: As you get closer to your intended destination, check the complexity of the terrain you're approaching and compare it to your earlier observations from maps and other larger-scale sources. Adjust your plans based on what you see.

SLOPE-SCALE (LOCAL) EVALUATION

Now that you have done both the regional-scale and mountain-scale (intermediate) evaluations, you're ready to zero in on a slope-scale (local) evaluation. This begins on the ground at the trailhead and does not end until you have exited avalanche terrain. Use all your senses. Pay attention. Keep talking and daydreaming to a minimum. Remember, in avalanche terrain we are all wild animals and not on the top of the food chain. Pay attention.

The Five Red Flags

You can tell a lot about the stability of the snowpack by simply looking for obvious clues. These are often known as the Five Red Flags. I list them below roughly in their order of importance. Yes, you have already considered many of them at the regional or mountain scale, but here you specifically look for them in your immediate area.

Caveat: deep slab avalanches and some persistent slabs won't exhibit many obvious clues, which makes them especially tricky.

1. Recent Avalanches

The best sign of avalanches are avalanches. The absolutely best, bull's-eye, top-of-the-list clue that a particular slope is dangerous is if you see a recent avalanche on a similar slope. It's such an obvious clue that many people miss it.

2. Recent Deposits of Wind-Drifted Snow

As I mentioned in Chapter 3, snow, like people, gets cranky with rapid change. Wind can deposit snow 10 times more rapidly than can snow that falls out of the sky, so usually wind is by far the most important weather factor to consider.

3. Recent New Snow

Added weight from snowstorms also plays a huge role—the more weight and the more quickly it's added, the more dangerous the conditions. Remember to think about *weight* of the snow, not the depth, because 5 centimeters (2 inches) of wet snow can weigh as much as 60 centimeters (2 feet) of very light snow.

4. Collapsing and Cracking (Audible Alarm Signals)

Collapsing snow (sometimes mistakenly called settlement) is when the snowpack collapses under you with a loud *whumpf.* (Actually, "whumpf" has been adopted as a technical term to describe collapsing snow.) As Alaska avalanche experts Jill Fredston and Doug Fesler say, *whumpf*ing or cracking is the "sound of Mother Nature screaming in your ear that the snowpack is unstable," and if there is a similar collapse on a slope that is steep enough to slide, it won't hesitate to do so.

Photo 4-2. Cracking snow is an obvious buzz from the avalanche rattlesnake. Don't take another step! Here, a 40-foot (12-meter) crack shoots out from my wife's skis. She was able to crack the fresh wind slab by safely standing on the flat of a ridge and watch the crack propagate below her. Luckily, the slope below is barely 30 degrees and is a good small test slope.

Collapsing snow occurs when your weight is enough to catastrophically collapse a buried weak layer, which is most commonly faceted snow or surface hoar. You can easily bring avalanches down from above in collapsing snow conditions. When the weak layer is already holding up the weight of a significant amount of snow and just the wimpy addition of your weight can collapse all the snow in sometimes a very large area, most people intuitively recognize this for a very dangerous situation. *Whump*fing almost always elicits a heart-thumping, wide-eyed look of terror. (It's interesting that seeing the scar of a recent avalanche doesn't produce the same response in most people, yet it's a much better indicator of danger.)

Cracking is another buzz from the avalanche rattlesnake. It means, "Don't take another step; stop and take stock of your surroundings." Cracking snow means that all the ingredients for an avalanche are present: not only has your weight over-loaded a buried weak layer, but the snowpack has stored enough elastic energy to propagate a crack. Once again, Mother Nature is hollering in your ear. Generally, the longer the crack the worse the situation. Make sure to stop. Poke around and see how well the slab is bonded to the underlying snow. We see cracking usu-ally in fresh wind slabs, but it can occur with most other kinds of instabilities. See Photo 4-2.

Photo 4-3. Roller balls (also called "pinwheels" or "snow snails") occur when dry snow becomes wet for the first time. They are usually a precursor to more serious wet avalanche danger. It's time to get off steep slopes.

5. Rapid Thaw

Snow gets cranky with rapid temperature changes, especially rapid warming. Always be suspicious of rapid warming of a cold, dry snowpack—especially rain falling on a cold, dry snowpack, which will almost always cause instant avalanching. Watch out for the first time meltwater percolates down through a previously cold, dry snowpack. Sometimes thaw problems can take longer. For instance, deep, wet slab avalanches on a persistent weak layer often occur after three days of percolating meltwater combined with no freezes at night.

Snowpack Tests

In addition to observations, you can test the stability of the snow in a number of ways without putting yourself at risk.

Volunteer Stability Testers

The mountains are increasingly filled with volunteer stability testers—skiers, snowmobilers, climbers, snowboarders, snowshoers, hunters, hikers, helicopter skiers, film crews, and Boy Scout troops, as well as falling cornices, falling seracs, and sluffs. Many of these handy volunteer stability testers seem to be more than willing to jump onto untracked slopes. If they make it without triggering an avalanche, then the chances are better that you will too—that's not guaranteed; remember, there are plenty of exceptions, but tracks are almost always better than no tracks. Also note how old the tracks are. The older the better, since that much more time has passed since the snowpack was loaded with weight. (In other words, the snowpack has had time to adjust to its load.)

There are few rules of thumb in the avalanche business, but one of them is this: If Joe Gnarly Powder Pig wants first tracks, let him have it. I always try to go last—never first. (See Chapter 5, Low-Risk Travel Rituals.) Never go first.

Caveat: Especially with a deeply buried, persistent weak layer, avalanches are difficult to trigger, so tracks on a slope mean very little in these conditions.

Ski Pole Test

When I travel with ski poles or an ice ax, I regularly push my pole or ax into the snow, feeling the unseen layers below. Most avalanche professionals do this hundreds of times per day. With hard snow, use the handle-end of the ski pole. Remember that we are dealing with the invisible here, so you are like a blind person. Use your white cane to "see" the unseen (see Photo 4-4). Simply push your pole down and feel for weak layers buried in the snow.

If I feel a lot of resistance in the surface layers and suddenly my pole drops through a layer that feels like mostly air, this usually means that a slab overlies a layer

Photo 4-4. When traveling, I probe with my ski pole hundreds of times a day to feel the unseen layers below. With harder snow, I turn my ski pole upside down. I often use my rescue probe to test layers and see the total depth of the snowpack. Avalanches are not mysterious or unpredictable, they are just invisible, hidden beneath the perfect façade.

of faceted snow or less dense snow (see Parts of a Slab Avalanche in Chapter 3), an especially dangerous combination. When I feel this, it's time to dig down and investigate further. Remember that the ski pole test gives you only a *general* feel for snowpack layering. It misses thin layers or subtle weak layers, such as surface hoar. When riding a snowmobile I can often feel the same buried weak layers by paying attention to the machine's track bogging down or punching through surface layers into weaker layers below. Realize, though, that it will not be nearly as sensitive or reliable a test as stopping and feeling with your hands.

Armpit Test

To test after a storm or for shallow weak layers, I do the armpit test dozens of times as I travel along. Dig out a small hole with your hand and then, on the uphill side, saw out a small square of snow with either your hand or the handle-end of a ski pole. Pull on this snow to see how well the surface slab is bonded to the underlying snow. See Photo 4-5.

Step Above the Track

You can do this test on skis, a snowboard, a snowmobile, or snowshoes. I occasionally step above the track and kick some surface snow onto the trail below. Or, climbing a slope on skis, at the apex of each switchback, I kick the snow and look for little slabs that pop out between the switchbacks.

Slope Cuts (aka Ski Cuts)

Ski cuts have been a standard technique among ski patrollers and helicopter ski guides for decades, but snowboarders and snowmobilers can do these tests as well, so instead I call them slope cuts. The idea is that if you might trigger an avalanche, you want to do it fully aware, with your speed built up, and heading for an island of safety. In theory, if the slope does fracture, your momentum will carry you off the moving slab, which helps minimize the chances of getting caught (see more details in Low-Risk Travel Rituals in Chapter 5).

Test Slopes

This is my favorite backcountry test. Find a small, steep slope where the consequences of a slide are small, such as a road cut or a small breakover in the slope. Look for something about 3–6 meters (10–20 feet) high. Then jump on the slope to see how it responds. If I get an avalanche on the test slope, I will definitely avoid any larger, more dangerous slopes with the same aspect and steepness. A test slope is a gift that you should never pass by without jumping on it (see Photo 4-6).

Photo 4-5. A quick test of surface layers: cut out a small block and tug on it.

Photo 4-6. I always like to hit small test slopes like this one to see how the snow responds. Yes, it's avalanche terrain, it's steep and wind loaded. But the consequences are quite low, which makes it a perfect test slope. It's much better to find out that the snow is unstable on this small slope than on the larger slope behind it. Remember, always have a partner waiting in a safe spot and always wear rescue gear.

Remember that even on small slopes, it's possible to get buried. Always have your partner watch from a safe spot.

Cornice Test

Cornices are the "bombs of the backcountry." Doing a cornice test is something that only advanced users should do. As you can well imagine, cornice tests can be very dangerous if done improperly. Yet they have been standard techniques for decades among ski patrollers, helicopter ski guides, and especially climbers. Basically, you find a cornice that weighs significantly more than a person and knock it down the slope.

First, do this test *only* if you are certain that no one is below you—very important. Most backcountry travelers would consider this test to be attempted homicide if someone is below. If you can't tell or the visibility is poor, don't do a cornice test. It is often very hard to see the entire slope below you while standing at the top, so look at the slope from another angle or use a spotter.

Photo 4-7. Trundling a cornice down the slope is an excellent stability test. 1) Make sure no one is below, 2) wear a belay rope, 3) cut something that weighs more than you (refrigerator size or larger), and 4) cut on a steep angle. You can use a snow saw mounted on the end of a ski pole, the other end of your belay rope (as shown), or a parachute cord with knots tied every foot or so.

A cornice the size of a refrigerator or a small car bouncing down a slope provides an excellent stability test. The smaller the cornice, the less effective the test. Look for small, fresh cornices, not large, old hard ones.

You can kick the cornice, shovel it, cut it with a snow saw mounted on the end of a ski pole, or—my preferred technique—either use your belay rope or a parachute cord with knots tied in it every foot or so, which act like teeth on a saw. Throw the cord over the cornice or push it over the edge with an avalanche probe. You can saw off a fairly large cornice in a minute or two. See Photo 4-7.

Make sure you cut with the snow saw or cord at a downward angle that is at least 40 degrees off the vertical plane. If you make your cut too flat, you will do a lot of huffing and puffing for nothing. The cornice will just sit there. This is also a great way to create a safe descent route during very unstable conditions. In other words, create an avalanche and use the slide path to descend.

Caveat: It doesn't take much imagination to see that knocking cornices down avalanche paths can be very dangerous. Again, make sure no one is below you! Practice the cornice test on safe slopes until you get the techniques worked out. Cornices have a nasty habit of breaking farther back than you think they should; *always* use a belay rope on slopes with bad consequences.

Snow-Pit Tests

Most of the time we can gather enough information about the snowpack without ever taking out the dreaded shovel. But sometimes the only way to get good information about deeper weak layers is to grease up your elbows and do some honest work. I almost always dig at least one or more snow pits in representative locations to get the general picture of what's going on in the snowpack.

I do not go into much detail here on the fine art of digging snow pits and all the various snow-pit tests you can do, but I will mention one quick, easy snow-pit test:

Extended Column Test: On the uphill wall of the snow pit, isolate a column of snow 90 centimeters wide and 30 centimeters deep (1 foot by 3 feet). You can use a snow saw mounted on a ski pole, but the best way to cut is with a cord and probe pole. (See Photo 4-8.)

On one end of the column, place your shovel on top, then tap with the palm of one hand on the shovel: 10 times articulating from the wrist, 10 times from the elbow, and 10 times from the shoulder; in each series of taps, tap harder and harder until you get a fracture in the snow.

Now comes the important part: Watch carefully to see if the fracture propagates all the way across the column. The statistics indicate that if the column both

Photo 4-8. Isolate a column of snow for an extended column test, a quick and easy way to assess the stability of the immediate snowpack.

initiates and propagates a fracture at the same time, it is an excellent indicator of instability regardless of how hard you have to tap to initiate the fracture. In this way, it's an either/or test. Either it propagates a fracture or it doesn't. In addition, the harder you have to tap indicates roughly how difficult the avalanche is to trigger.

You can do this test on a flat slope as well, but it's best to do all snow-pit tests on a slope similar in aspect and steepness to the slope you are trying to forecast in order to match the snowpack characteristics closely. This test has been well proven in different climates, and has a lower false-positive rate than any other kind of test.

SNOWPACK HAZARD

After testing the snowpack, professional backcountry avalanche forecasters determine the avalanche danger rating by considering both probability and consequence (Figure 4-3). We can use this diagram as a conceptual way to understand

Figure 4-3. An avalanche danger rating is based on both the likelihood of triggering an avalanche and the avalanche size. This is a standard probability-consequence diagram used in many risk management fields. The specific danger rating for each combination is not filled in here because the danger ratings can vary by the type of avalanche and the application.

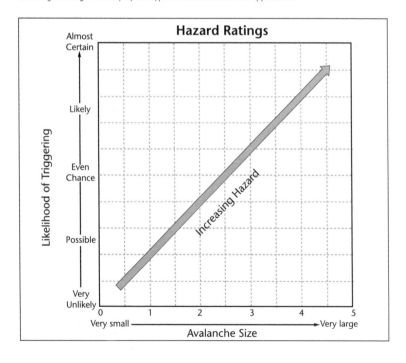

hazard. It shows that the snowpack hazard is determined by the combination between likelihood of triggering and expected size of the avalanche.

On the vertical axis is the likelihood of triggering an avalanche, which is based on the snowpack's sensitivity to human triggers and the distribution of the human-triggered potential. Although there is no strict definition for likelihood, most forecasters seem to calibrate it as the estimated likelihood of a human-triggered avalanche occurring on a specific slope where a group is doing laps for the day. It's calibrated for travelers like skiers, snowboarders, snowshoers, and climbers. If you are on a snowmobile, realize that a snowmobile with a person onboard exerts two-and-a-half to five times the amount of stress on buried weak layers than a person alone, so snowmobilers may be a notch higher on the likelihood scale than a skier. Pay attention to the avalanche advisory to see what kind of activity was reported from the previous day, both from the backcountry and from explosive-triggered avalanches. Also notice what kind of avalanche activity others are triggering or that you trigger using test slopes and cornice tests.

On the horizontal scale is the size or severity of the avalanche. Avalanche professionals rank avalanche size on a scale of one to five based on the amount of

TABLE 4-1. AVALANCHE SIZE

Size	Destructive Force	Typical Types of Avalanches and Severity of Avalanches
1	Not enough to bury a person except in a terrain trap	Loose snow sluffs (8–15 cm x 3 m) (3–6" x 10') Shallow, small, soft slabs (8 cm x 3 m) (3" x 10') Avalanches considered to be "manageable"; good candidates for slope cuts
2	Enough to bury or injure a person or break small trees	Typical soft slabs (30 cm x 9 m) (1' x 30') Shallow hard slabs (15 cm x 9 m) (6" x 30') Typical human-triggered avalanches; some are too large for slope cuts except in low-consequence terrain
3	Can break trees or destroy a house—high likelihood of injury or death	Larger soft slabs (60–90 cm x 60 m) (2'–3' x 200') Medium-size hard slabs (30–60 cm x 60 m) (1'–2' x 200') Large, human-triggered avalanches; quite deadly. These are "unmanageable" avalanches. You must avoid them.
4	Can destroy an acre of trees or a building—almost certain injury or death	Deep slabs, both soft and hard (1 m x 180 m) (4' x 600') Typically run to historic run-out distance Can be difficult for humans to trigger; if humans are caught in them, they are usually unsurvivable.
5	Largest avalanches— can destroy a village— almost certain injury or death	Deep slabs, both soft or hard (2 m x 610 m) (6' x 2000') Often the entire starting zone will release and the resulting avalanche will overrun historic run-out distance. These are usually unsurvivable.

mass in the avalanche. Note the kind of avalanches expected (or recently occurring) and refer to the information in Table 4-1.

SNOW STABILITY CHECKLIST

The theme of this book is to use a system to manage risk in backcountry avalanche terrain. This step-by-step checklist answers the question: how dangerous is the snowpack? I list factors in chronological order of how we usually come to the decision, as well as scale: from the large regional scale working down to an intermediate mountain scale to the local slope scale.

SNOWPACK STABILITY CHECKLIST

Here is a checklist of important observations and tests:

REGIONAL SCALE—PRETRIP PLANNING

First, start with the big picture.

- ☐ Avalanche advisory: What is the overall danger rating?
- ☐ What kind of avalanche dragon(s) are we dealing with?
    - ❖ What is the pattern? (aspect, elevation, terrain type, steepness)
    - ❖ How do I recognize it?
    - ❖ How do I manage it?
- ☐ What kind of avalanche activity has occurred? What's the pattern?
- ☐ What is the weather forecast?
    - ❖ What's the pattern?
    - ❖ Is the weather making the snowpack more dangerous or less dangerous?
- ☐ What kind of partners can I choose?

➤ Critical decision point: What's the general destination for today?

SNOWPACK STABILITY CHECKLIST (CONTINUED)

MOUNTAIN SCALE (INTERMEDIATE SCALE)—TRAVELING TO THE DESTINATION

Once we have made the big-picture decisions, we focus on the intermediate, mountain-size scale.

☐ Red flags:
  ❖ Recent avalanches?
  ❖ Collapsing and cracking?
  ❖ Recent wind?
  ❖ Recent snow?
  ❖ Recent thaw?
☐ What kind of weather and visibility will I have?

➤ Critical decision point: Which slopes are the possible, safe choices for today?

SLOPE SCALE (LOCAL SCALE)—APPROACHING OR ON THE SLOPES OF CHOICE

Now comes the fun part but also the most-critical decisions. Pay attention. This is where we bet with our life.

☐ Red flags in the immediate area:
  ❖ Recent avalanches?
  ❖ Collapsing and cracking?
  ❖ Recent wind?
  ❖ Recent snow?
  ❖ Recent thaw?
☐ Tests:
  ❖ Test slopes?
  ❖ Volunteer stability testers? (Are others triggering avalanches?)
  ❖ Cornice tests?
  ❖ Armpit tests for new snow instability?
  ❖ Snow-pit tests for deeper weak layers?

➤ Critical decision point: Do we bet with our life?

None of us would ever cross a busy street without looking both ways. Yet when faced with the complexity and uncertainty of avalanches, many victims simply roll the dice and bet with their life. We can never prevent all avalanche accidents, but the step-by-step system presented in this chapter, as well as in the rest of the book, can prevent most of them. Thus, we can have low-risk fun in avalanche terrain. Knowledge is power; knowledge is powder.

TAKE-HOME POINT

When analyzing snowpack, don't get married on the first date. You need to meet the parents, paddle a canoe together for a couple weeks, travel to a third world country together—in other words, gather lots of information from a variety of sources. Remember this is a critical decision; you are betting with your very life. Be sure to work your way through the checklist (or at least the condensed checklist, Figure 9-9) before making this potentially life-changing or life-ending decision.

CHAPTER 5

LOW-RISK TRAVEL RITUAL

When I first started working on the ski patrol at Bridger Bowl Ski Area in Montana 35 years ago, I learned several rules I was to never violate when running avalanche control routes. I call them the Richmond Rules because my old ski-racing buddy, Doug Richmond, taught them to me, but of course, he had learned from his mentors. Day after day, he would drill the rules into me, and he would dole out the punishment when I failed to follow them. He took the rules seriously, and in later years I could see why. In almost every instance in which an avalanche professional had died, if that person had been following these rules, he or she would probably still be alive. The Richmond Rules have saved my life several times. I have modified and expanded upon Doug's original rules through the years to their present form. They are so important that I consider them the Ten Commandments of safe travel.

TEN COMMANDMENTS OF LOW-RISK TRAVEL

Even the cagiest avalanche professional in the world is still a human being, and humans make mistakes. We will all make the wrong decision at least once in our life—more likely several times. Professionals tend to get caught when they let their guard down and either underestimate the hazard or overestimate their skills. But when we make our inevitable mistakes, we had better be practicing many of these commandments of low-risk travel, because they can help to mitigate the consequences.

These commandments are not something we do only when we think conditions are dangerous. We do them consistently. Low-risk travel is more than a technique, it's a ritual. It works only if you do it *all* the time. It's our habits that save our life.

1st Commandment: Thou Shalt Go One at a Time—and Leave Someone in a Safe Spot to Do the Rescue

Resist the herding instinct. The feeling of safety-in-numbers is hardwired into the human brain, and for good reason. For millions of years, it has been a good defense against lions and tigers and bears—but it has just the opposite effect on avalanche dragons. It's essential to resist the herding instinct for the following reasons:

- ❖ If something does go wrong, you *always* need to have someone left in a safe spot to dig the other(s) out.
- ❖ Groups of people weigh more than a single person and are more likely to overload buried weak layers.
- ❖ Several people wandering all over the slope are much more likely to find the trigger point of an avalanche than a single person.

Small groups: Expose only one person to the hazard at a time.

Larger groups: Spread out or split the group in half. Always leave enough people in a safe place so they can carry out a rescue. Sometimes it's better to keep two smaller groups on two different slopes in visual contact than to have two groups on different parts of the same slope.

No matter the size of your group, stay in visual, voice, or radio contact.

Corollary 1: Never Cross above Your Partner
Some ski patrols consider crossing above your partner tantamount to attempted homicide. If you trigger an avalanche on top of your partner, it's not only a very nasty behavior but there's also a good chance that *both* of you will get killed, because no one is left to carry out a rescue. In avalanche terrain, you should only travel above your partner after you get their permission. Among pros, you will often hear them say, "I need to cross above you. Are you in a good spot?" And sometimes the lower person might say, "Wait a minute. Let me duck under that big tree over there." Or, "Maybe I should cross first to that island of safety, and you can follow in my track after I signal you to cross." And so on.

Obviously, when traveling uphill people are often stacked above others, but you usually choose safer terrain while doing this, such as a gentler ridge or thick trees. I cringe every time I see people put a climbing track in prime avalanche terrain because you need extremely stable conditions to get away with exposing so many people at once. For snowmobilers, the rule is never go up to help your buddy get unstuck. Better to keep an eye on him from a safe spot.

Descending on skis or snowboards is also tricky. Usually one person exposes themselves to the hazard at a time and waits in an "island of safety" before they signal, shout, or radio the next person to come down.

Also be careful that your "island of safety" is really safe. All too often, someone will descend halfway and while waiting for a partner to descend will wait in a thicker grove of trees or on a small spur ridge that is only slightly safer than standing out in

Figure 5-1. These two skiers are betting with their lives that the snow is extremely stable. If not, this would be a difficult avalanche to survive because of the cliffs and rocks—this photo shows only the top quarter of a very long avalanche path. At least they are somewhat spread out, but the trailing skier stands on a "false island of safety." The trailing skier should wait back under the earlier rock buttress until the lead skier gets to the ridge.

the middle of the slope. This can happen, reversed, on the way up the slope (Figure 5-1). Sometimes these false islands of safety are overrun by an avalanche triggered by the person above. So if you can't get into a good safe spot, it's probably better to descend all the way to the bottom and get completely out of the way.

Corollary 2: Get Out of the Way at the Bottom
All too often, people stop halfway down or at the bottom of the slope and pull out their camera. Or snowmobilers doing hill climbing will gather at the bottom with a good view of the slope, and an avalanche will overrun the whole group. Be sure to wait well outside the avalanche run-out area.

2nd Commandment: Thou Shalt Have an Escape Route Preplanned
If you trigger an avalanche when you're just standing in the middle of the avalanche path (or you get your snowmobile stuck on the slope), you have almost no chance to escape off the moving slab.

Everyone should use slope cuts, but the first person across the slope especially should always practice them. See Slope Cuts (aka Ski Cuts) in Chapter 4.

Skiers' and snowboarders' slope cut technique for getting off the slab: Beginning at the top of a slope, cross the slope rapidly at about a 45-degree angle, aiming for safer terrain such as a gentler slope, a rock outcropping, or a grove of dense trees.

Snowmobilers' slope cut technique for getting off the slab: Unlike skiers and 'boarders, snowmobilers have the ability to slope cut from the bottom. Instead of doing your first hill climb up the middle of the slope, either climb off to the side or do a swooping, traversing climb low on the slope where you can get off the slope in a hurry if it does break. If you fracture the slope while going uphill and you can't get off to the side, just grab some throttle and keep heading up in hopes that most of the snow will pass beneath you. If you fracture the slope on the way down and can't get off to the side, your only choice is to try to outrun the avalanche, which might work for small avalanches but probably won't for the big ones. Often snowmobilers get thrown off their sled when they hit the stauchwall (the bottom boundary of a slab where it rides up over the snow below) of a large avalanche.

Slope Cut Caveats

Slope cuts are much less effective for hard or deep slabs. Although slope cuts work better for soft, shallow slabs, nevertheless, you should still practice slope cuts on hard slabs as a good defensive technique. Just realize that especially with deep, hard slabs, the third or tenth person across the slope is nearly as likely to trigger the slab as the first one across.

Slope cuts are best used as a defensive technique not to intentionally trigger known hazards. Don't get cocky just because you've successfully cut a few avalanches and escaped. Slope cuts are not a guarantee; they're only one more tool in your bag of tricks to push the safety arrow a little closer to 100 percent.

Keep your speed up. Slope cuts depend on momentum to take you off the slab. Snowmobilers should avoid getting bogged down during a hill climb. When you are on skis or a snowboard, don't poke along like a cow—make like an antelope.

Don't get caught on the leading edge. Inexperienced people tend to cut too low on the slope and are therefore caught in the leading edge—the most dangerous part—of an avalanche.

Sluff Management Techniques

People who ski, snowboard, snowmobile, or climb in extreme terrain constantly have to deal with sluffs and small slabs. Since the terrain is so steep, even small amounts of sluffing snow can knock you off your feet and send you for a nasty ride.

Photo 5-1. If you have to cross a suspect slope, stay high on the avalanche path so there is a minimum of snow above you. This is an intentionally triggered avalanche high on Mount Foraker in Alaska. Getting caught here would involve a 10,000-vertical-foot ride that would ruin your day. © Greg Collins

First, here are some techniques for managing sluffs:

- ❖ As you descend, try to move across the fall line instead of straight up or down.
- ❖ Never turn back into a moving sluff.
- ❖ Use small subridges (spines and flutes) to your advantage. Stay on or near the crests.
- ❖ When you drop into the gullies, stay up on the sides, avoid crossing the bottom of the gully when the sluffs you have kicked off will be traveling.
- ❖ When one drainage fills up with sluffing snow, you can often switch into a fresh drainage to your left or right until it fills up with too much snow; then switch again to a fresh slope.

Second, sluffs tend to go slowly at first, but when they reach a certain critical mass, they jump into warp speed and rocket down the mountain, which can take an inexperienced person by surprise.

Third, go either slower than the sluff or faster than the sluff. To go slower than the sluff, make a turn or two and wait for it to run out ahead of you. With the new

Photo 5-2. A good example of sluff management. This skier is staying along the crest of the spine and switching to a new spine if things build up too much. Be sure to glance over your shoulder every few turns to see what is chasing you. © Scott Markewitz

wide skis and snowboards, many of the more elite athletes can stay out ahead of the sluff, but the most important part is to look over your shoulder every turn or two to keep an eye out for sluffs catching up to you from behind.

Managing sluffs takes experience and skill. Start practicing in terrain with fewer bad consequences before you jump in big time, where sluffs can kill you if you don't know what you're doing.

Corollary 1: Cross High on the Avalanche Path

If you trigger an avalanche, you want to be as high as possible on the slab, for several reasons:

❖ Snow below you can't bury you, but the snow above you can.

❖ The closer you are to the trailing edge of the avalanche (the upper edge of the moving debris) the more likely it is that you will be left behind on the bed surface or not buried too deeply if you take the full ride. "Avalanches die from the tail," as the Swiss scientist Perry Bartlett puts it. In other words, avalanches lose mass from the tail, or trailing edge, which causes the avalanche to slow and ultimately stop.

Corollary 2: Turn Around or Dig In

Remember, you can always go back the way you came. The route that got you there will almost always get you back.

When all else fails, go underground. Many people have saved themselves during storms by digging a snow cave or creating a snow shelter, which can be surprisingly warm and cozy. Yes, you might be uncomfortable and your loved ones may worry, but at least you will be alive.

3rd Commandment: Thou Shalt Never Go First

Yes, I'm being hyperbolic here to make a point. You should never test the stability of a slope using your most valuable possession: your life. Your parents have invested thousands of dollars in you, and it makes no sense to risk that kind of investment, especially when there seems to be an endless supply of volunteer stability testers willing to work for free. Other snowboarders, skiers, snowshoers, snowmobilers, hikers, Boy Scout troops—they all seem eager for the job.

According to Swiss statistics, 90 percent of avalanche accidents are triggered by the first person down. In other words, the more tracks on a slope, the better. (In intermountain or continental climates, I suspect the proportion is much lower.)

I love going last. All my friends are starting to get wise to me because I have a million excuses. I'll stand at the top and fiddle with my bindings, start chomping on my lunch, call someone on the phone—I'll do anything except go first.

Photo 5-3. Cornices often break much farther back than you would expect. Never walk up to the edge of a drop-off in the mountains. This mountain guide in Canada who went too close got lucky and narrowly escaped being pulled over the edge. © Mike Welch Photography

When you do go down the slope, follow other people's tracks, spooning your tracks in with theirs. Treat an avalanche slope like a minefield. If someone else successfully crossed a particular spot without triggering an avalanche, you probably can cross safely there too. This is one instance in which the herding instinct works to our advantage.

If you can't find any volunteers, you can use an involuntary stability tester—a cornice, for example. Just tumble a large chunk of cornice down the slope first (see Snowpack Tests in Chapter 4 for more details).

4th Commandment: Thou Shalt Never Trust a Cornice

I have personally had three very close calls with cornices, and I'm deeply frightened of them. **Never, never, never walk up to the edge of a drop-off** without first checking it out from another angle to see if you'll be standing on nothing but air. If you can't check it out, don't go to the edge without being belayed by a rope. All too many otherwise sensible people have been needlessly killed this way. When you're traveling along a corniced ridge, it's obvious enough that you should travel on the upwind side, but a lot of people travel too close and suddenly get the big elevator ride to hell. Most old-time mountaineers have a cornice story or two.

Cornices have a nasty habit of breaking farther back than you expect; I have seen cornices break farther back than I would have ever imagined. A cornice once broke away behind a line of trees and a large bush that stood between the edge and me. I wore a brace on my knee for a month because of that very close call.

Also remember that a person plus a large cornice tumbling down a slope together make a terrific avalanche trigger. Treat cornices with respect; use a belay rope when possible.

Cornices are not all bad. You can use them as a stability test. (See the Cornice Test in Chapter 4.)

5th Commandment: Thou Shalt Be Obsessed with Consequences

What will happen if it slides? What's below you? What's above you? What is the slope connected to? If you don't like the consequences, maybe you should find

Photo 5-4. This is terrain with zero tolerance for error—4000 vertical feet with plenty of cliffs, rocks, and trees. Three snowboarders died on the big path in the middle right when they took runs on the lower apron during a very large snowstorm. The avalanche released from above. There were 14 people on the slope at the time. This slope has always been an attractive hazard because there is a popular parking lot nearby.

Photo 5-5. Always practice democratic communication. Listen to everyone's ideas, make a plan, and make sure everyone knows the plan. Repeat often.

another option. Remember that unsurvivable terrain requires extremely stable snow conditions. No exceptions.

Always look for the downside of any decision, and always challenge your assumptions and beliefs. Continually ask yourself: "Why might this be wrong?"

6th Commandment: Thou Shalt Start Small and Work Your Way Up

Terrain almost always gives you small gifts—small test slopes—that you can jump on to see how they respond. Never pass up a test slope. It's better to find out the stability of the snowpack on small slopes that won't kill you before you get to the big ones that might. Only a fool jumps into a big slope without first gathering a lot of data from other safer places.

Starting small is a standard technique for helicopter skiing operations. They start on gentler, safer slopes and work slowly into more dangerous terrain. Sometimes it takes several days to gather enough evidence to be able to commit to terrain with very dangerous consequences. The extreme videos never show that part.

7th Commandment: Thou Shalt Communicate

Even in the Information Age, communication—or lack of it—remains the central problem of our lives. Have you ever noticed that if people would just talk honestly with each other, it would eliminate the vast majority of television and movie plots? It would also prevent most wars.

Professional ski patrols have very strict rules about communication when running an avalanche control route. First, you always need to be in voice or radio contact with your partner. Second, you give clear commands: "You stay on the ridge, and I'm going to do a ski cut to the rocks. After I get there, I'll wave that I'm okay and you come across. Got that?" Or, "I'm going to ski down and around the corner under the cliff; stay here until I call on the radio when I'm safe, and you should follow my tracks down and join me."

I love going into the backcountry with other pros because we have all learned the system and operate according to the system. Everything else seems chaotic and dangerous. I also like to use personal radios to communicate because safety comes from being spread out but also being able to communicate. Plus, it's easy to get separated when descending through trees on skis or snowboards or when traveling on a snowmobile. With a radio, you can find one another. Remember mobile phones often don't have service in the backcountry.

Communication should not be like a military operation in which orders come from the top down but, rather, all decisions and communications should be made democratically and with as much information as possible.

Photo 5-6. I often carry a lightweight belay rope (also called a rando rope) for use in high-consequence terrain especially around cornices, to dig a snow profile or do a slope cut.

8th Commandment: Thou Shalt Use a Belay Rope

Many serious avalanche professionals carry and use a belay rope. I often carry a 30 meters of 7-mm rope. You can use a belay rope for digging a snow pit on a suspect slope, rappeling past obstacles, slope cutting, kicking or sawing cornices, waiting for an explosive to go off when standing in an insecure spot, or carrying out a rescue. Ropes are good. Carry one, especially when conditions are dodgy.

9th Commandment: Thou Shalt Use the Right Equipment

Based on many anecdotal examples of victims with releasable ski bindings ending up on the surface and those without them ending up buried, for many years, avalanche professionals doing avalanche control have required releasable bindings and forbidden straps on ski poles. Being tumbled in an avalanche or strained through trees with objects attached to your limbs just doesn't seem like a good idea. Every year many fatalities occur from someone simply falling head first into a tree well or the bottom of a steep gully, where releasable bindings could have allowed that person to escape. Even breakaway pole straps can be dangerous because they may prevent you from grabbing an air-bag trigger or Avalung mouthpiece or getting your hands near your face so that you can form an air pocket before the debris comes to a stop. The ski patrol made me cut off my pole straps years ago and I haven't used them since.

Bring the standard rescue equipment of a beacon, shovel, and probe, but also consider an avalanche air bag as your first choice to further increase survivability. They are very effective and, statistically, they work better than beacons. Those who can afford the extra expense and weight of an avalanche air bag should use one. As they have become lighter and cheaper, they are now considered standard equipment, like wearing a personal floatation device (PFD) on a white-water river. You should also consider wearing an Avalung and a RECCO (locator) chip somewhere on your body. Both are cheap and lightweight, so there is no reason not to use them. (See Chapter 8, Rescue Technology, for details.)

Everyone should wear a helmet. Most trauma deaths among avalanche victims involve head and neck injuries that might be prevented by wearing a helmet.

Here are some sport-specific equipment recommendations:

Snowmobilers: Always wear a helmet with a face shield. It helps protect you from trauma, and at least in smaller avalanches, the helmet may not fill up with snow.

Snowmobilers should also carry a shovel, a probe, and other rescue gear on their back in a small pack (preferably an air-bag pack) instead of on the snowmobile. If you survive and your snowmobile is buried, you will need a shovel to dig out your friends.

Skiers: Always wear releasable bindings and do not use pole straps. There is good anecdotal evidence and some data that indicate that victims with releasable bindings tend to end up on the surface significantly more often than victims with skis (or a snowboard or snowshoes) attached.

The Ten Essentials

I almost always carry these Ten Essentials to make sure I can (1) respond positively to an accident or emergency and (2) safely spend a night outdoors if necessary. Additional useful equipment includes a radio to communicate with your partner(s), a mobile phone, and an inclinometer to measure slope steepness. And don't forget to bring a hot thermos on a cold day.

1. Navigation: a compass or GPS device (or smartphone with compass and GPS apps)
2. Sun protection: sunglasses, sunscreen
3. Insulation: extra warm clothes—a minimum of extra hat, mittens, puff coat, and pants
4. Illumination: headlamp
5. First-aid supplies
6. Fire: matches, lighter, firestarter
7. Repair kit: pocket knife, tools
8. Nutrition: extra food—and chocolate! You gotta have chocolate
9. Hydration: extra water or means to melt snow for water
10. Emergency shelter: lightweight space blanket or a couple of large orange garbage bags

10th Commandment: Thou Shalt Remember—Terrain, Terrain, Terrain

As Canadian avalanche consultant Chris Stethem says, "Never underestimate the importance or subtlety of terrain. It takes a lifetime to learn terrain—maybe two lifetimes." If you learn nothing else from this book, become a master of terrain management on both a large and a small scale. Continually choose a route, both going up and coming down, based on steepness and consequences, anchors, aspect with respect to the wind and sun, and slope shape. (See Chapter 2, How Dangerous Is the Terrain?)

TAKE-HOME POINT

Low-risk travel is more than a technique. It should become ritual: it works only if you do it *all* the time. Good habits save lives.

CHAPTER 6

OOPS—SURVIVAL STRATEGIES

As we saw in Chapter 5, we can often recover from the inevitable mistakes we make by practicing the low-risk travel ritual, which deals with the exposure part of the risk equation (see Figure 9-1 in chapter 9). But when those measures don't work, we depend on survival and rescue strategies, which address the final term in the risk equation: vulnerability. In other words, when things go seriously wrong, how do we minimize the damage?

It's true that good avalanche skills can prevent most avalanche incidents. But we have to remember that whenever we work in the mediums of snow and weather, which are inherently variable and uncertain, our risk reduction measures might not work as well as we would like to believe. Stuff happens. In addition, we are all human and we all regularly make mistakes. Thus, anyone who spends much time in avalanche terrain will eventually either experience an avalanche in their own party or will come upon one that has happened to another party. Many people have been saved by avalanche rescue, so it's essential that we maximize the chances for survival by preparing for the worst.

STRATEGY FOR AVALANCHE VICTIMS

Most people don't make it off a moving slab avalanche. Everything happens *very* fast (see Table 6-1), and unless you are practicing a slope cut or already have an escape route preplanned and have been rehearsing everything in your mind, you most likely won't be able to do it. Most people don't even know what's going on until it's too late. If you are caught in an avalanche, some of these techniques may work.

While the Avalanche Is Moving

Remember, you have at most five seconds to take the steps below before the avalanche is moving so fast that you will be disoriented and unable to be proactive.

TABLE 6-1. TIMETABLE FOR A TYPICAL AVALANCHE	
Time	What to Expect If Caught
Fracture begins	You may hear a muffled *whumpf* sound, sometimes a loud *crack*. You notice cracks in the snow around you.
1 to 2 seconds	The slab starts to move. It feels like someone pulled the rug out from under you. Most people fall down. The slab shatters into blocks. The slab quickly picks up speed and after 2 seconds is moving about 15 km/hr (10 mph). In other words, in order to escape off the slab, you need to take action *now*. After the first 2 seconds, it may be too late. If you haven't preplanned your escape route, you probably won't be able to pull it off. This is the time to pull the rip cord on your avalanche air bag, bite down on your Avalung mouthpiece, or grab a tree.
2 to 5 seconds	The avalanche is moving 15 to 40 km/hr (10 to 30 mph). The blocks are now tumbling furiously. Skiing, snowboarding, and snowmobiling become impossible. Ski bindings release. It's now too late to grab a tree because you're definitely moving fast enough that an impact with a tree will cause injury or death. After this, you are, as Doug Richmond says, "a fly in the toilet bowl."
5 to 10 seconds	The avalanche is traveling 70 to 130 km/hr (40 to 80 mph). You are being tumbled hard and do not know which way is up. With every breath, you suck in a snow-air mixture that forms a plug of ice in your throat. Breathing is difficult. Hats, mittens, goggles are gone.
10 to 15 seconds	The avalanche slows down and the debris solidifies into a cohesive block even well before it comes to a complete stop. If you don't have an Avalung, make sure you bury your mouth in the crook of your elbow to make an air pocket.
Avalanche stops	Debris instantly sets up like concrete, often while it is still moving. You are frozen into place and cannot move. Completely buried victims cannot dig themselves out or form an air pocket.
4 minutes	As you rebreathe the carbon dioxide that builds up in the snow around your mouth, you begin to lose consciousness.
15 minutes	Fewer than half of those buried will still be alive but unconscious.
25 minutes	70% of completely buried victims not already killed by trauma will be dead.
35 minutes	90% of completely buried victims not already killed by trauma will be dead. Anyone who survives after this time must have an air pocket, which slows the buildup of carbon dioxide.

Yell

Let your partners know that you are caught: yell as loud as you can.

Note: Some folks are what we call "hooters"—they like to hoot and holler as they ski, snowboard, or snowmobile their way down a slope to let everyone know how much fun they are having. Save the yelling for when you need it. Besides, most of us go to the backcountry for peace and quiet. It's just bad form to make a racket in a quiet place.

Try to Escape Off the Slab

Remember that the snow below you can't bury you, but the snow above you can. So do whatever it takes to let as much snow pass below you as possible. Even if you still get taken for the full ride, at least some of these techniques give you a chance to be on the slower, trailing edge of the avalanche where you stand a much better chance of ending up on the surface:

❖ If you are able, use your momentum or the power of the snowmobile to move toward the edge of the avalanche, where you can ride onto non-moving or slower-moving snow.

❖ If you are near the upper fracture line of the slab, sometimes you can climb uphill, dig into the bed surface, and self arrest.

❖ Try to grab a tree if you can. Do it very quickly. Once the avalanche gains speed, a tree becomes a dangerous obstacle.

If You Can't Get Off the Slab, Get Rid of Your Equipment

Release your ski bindings. Skis with releasable bindings will be torn off quickly, but snowboards and snowshoes don't have releasable bindings, which is a big problem. Some 'boarders rig their bindings with a rip cord to get out of them in an avalanche.

Leave Your Pack On

You should leave your pack on for the following reasons:

❖ A pack provides valuable padding to your back and kidneys when you're bouncing off trees and rocks.

❖ Should you survive, your pack contains everything you'll need: shovel, probe, extra hat, mittens and warm clothes, food, water, first-aid kit, etc.

❖ Larger objects tend to end up on the surface, similar to the way you shake a bag of tortilla chips to get the largest pieces to the top. Your pack helps make you a larger object, which will help keep you near the surface.

Deploy Avalanche Gear If You Have Any

- ❖ Get your Avalung mouthpiece in your mouth, if you have an Avalung. (See Avalung section in Chapter 8, Rescue Technology.)
- ❖ Deploy your avalanche air bag if you have one. (See Avalanche Air Bags section in Chapter 8, Rescue Technology.)

To Swim or Not to Swim

Every avalanche instructor since the beginning of time has instructed their students to "swim" hard to stay on the surface of the avalanche. Since riding in avalanche debris feels very similar to floating through a rapid in a river, those who know how to swim will likely swim anyway.

Much of the avalanche moves in "granular flow": larger objects rise to the surface through "inverse segregation." And it's a good thing for us, because the human body is three times denser than snow, so if avalanches flowed like water, we would instantly sink to the bottom. Instead, most buried avalanche victims are within the top meter (3 feet) of the snow surface, and deeper burials usually occur only in terrain traps such as gullies.

Although some articles have been written that question the wisdom of swimming in avalanche debris, avalanche scientists agree that there is no data to support the idea that you should not swim. But everyone does agree that you should never swim at the expense of protecting your airway, especially as the avalanche slows. Far too many victims are found dead, frozen in swimming motions. Which brings us to our next point.

As the Avalanche Slows Down

As avalanche debris slows down, friction tends to cause the leading debris to pile up in front, and large areas of debris often solidify into a solid mass even before the avalanche comes to a complete stop.

With One Arm, Make an Air Space Around Your Mouth

Avalanche victims often report that they were frozen in place much sooner than they expected—even while the avalanche was still moving. It's important to make an air pocket in front of your mouth as the avalanche slows down.

If you don't have an Avalung, make sure to bury your mouth in the crook of one arm by reaching across your face and grabbing your pack strap by your opposite shoulder, even as you continue to struggle with your other limbs. The larger the cavity around your mouth, the longer you will live under the snow. If you can exhale your carbon dioxide along your arm after you're buried, you will last longer than if your mouth is in direct contact with the snow. Plus, protecting your mouth in the crook of your arm helps prevent the formation of an impermeable ice mask, which exacerbates buildup of carbon dioxide near your mouth.

Snowmobilers: A helmet with a full face mask seems to help prevent the formation of an ice mask, at least in smaller avalanches. In larger avalanches, the helmet is often filled with snow or the mask flips up. Even if you're wearing a helmet with a face mask, it's probably best to practice the same technique described above.

Extend a Hand Toward the Surface

You might not even know which way is up, but still try to push a hand toward what you think is the surface. It's much easier to find a victim by spotting a visible body part than it is by using a beacon or probe. But make sure your other arm is covering your mouth.

Remember you must protect your mouth and extend your other hand to the surface *well before* the avalanche comes to a complete stop, because often the debris seizes up as it's still moving.

When the Avalanche Comes to a Stop

Once the avalanche stops, it will set up firmly. Often, you can hardly move a finger, unless you are very near the surface or the debris is unusually soft—for example, in a very small avalanche.

Relax

Relax. Right! Even Zen masters will have a hard time relaxing after all that. But remember that the clock is ticking until your exhaled carbon dioxide builds up to the point that it puts you to sleep, so do your best to go into hibernation mode. You won't be able to move anyway, so you will not have much choice.

If you're lucky enough to have a hand above or very near the surface, you may be able to move snow, which could help to create a channel to disperse your carbon dioxide. But don't overexert in this kind of effort; you'll simply increase your carbon dioxide output. The vast majority of completely buried victims quickly lose consciousness.

TAKE-HOME POINT

In 2 seconds an avalanche is moving at about 16 kilometers per hour (10 miles per hour). In 5 seconds it is moving at up to 50 kilometers per hour (30 miles per hour), and in 10 seconds it is moving at up to 130 kilometers per hour (80 miles per hour). In 15 seconds it stops moving and sets up like concrete. If you are trapped under the snow, you will quickly suffocate.

STRATEGY FOR NON-BURIED COMPANIONS

You have just lived your basic nightmare: You have just watched your partner, friend, or loved one trigger an avalanche, get swept away, and vanish in the debris. Now that person's survival depends only on you!

In stressful situations like this, the brain's frontal lobe (the site of your logic and judgment) usually shuts down, and you operate at an impaired level. Like everyone else in these situations, you will make stupid mistakes. Even rescues by professionals are often a mess. When the guacamole hits the fan, everyone operates on autopilot, and the more you have practiced beforehand, the more likely your autopilot will make the right choices. Practice, practice, practice. It's the only way to do a rescue quickly. People who don't practice regularly often fail to find victims in time to save their lives.

Try to Watch the Last-Seen Area

If you can see the victims, watch them closely as they are swept away. Memorize exactly where you saw them last, and watch them as they travel down the mountain to see where they end up. If they are swallowed up by snow, watch the parcel of snow to see where it ends up.

Often the victims travel straight down the flow line from their last-seen area, and clues such as gloves and hats that float to the surface also line up with the victim. Knowing approximately where to start searching makes things go much faster.

Send Someone for Help?

1. An avalanche victim is essentially a drowning victim. Time is of the essence. In most backcountry settings, a rescue crew won't show up for an hour or two, even in the best of circumstances. By that time, the rescue operation will likely have turned into a body recovery. You need all your resources to stay and help get your friend(s) out of the snow and breathing as soon as possible.

2. As a general rule of thumb, if you feel that you can complete the rescue in less than 15 minutes, then you should not delay the rescue by calling 911 or sending someone for help (in the absence of any electronic communication). Also, the victim might not even need help, in which case, you don't want to unnecessarily endanger the lives of rescuers. If you have a lot of people available to do the rescue, you can consider designating one person to handle electronic communications to at least notify rescuers that their services might be needed and you will call them back as soon as you know more details.

Keep Track of Witnesses and Survivors

If you didn't see the accident but others did, keep close track of those witnesses. Witnesses have a wealth of valuable information that you need in order to speed up the rescue; plus, witnesses and survivors are often in a difficult emotional state and need someone to keep track of them. Witnesses, especially frantic witnesses, have a tendency to bolt off to call for a rescue party, wander away from the scene—perhaps into the next avalanche path—or interfere with the rescue efforts. Sit them down. Calm them down. Ask them:

- ❖ How many people were in the party?
- ❖ Were they all wearing beacons?
- ❖ Exactly where did they last see the victim(s)?

These are all critical questions that only the witnesses or survivors can answer. Many rescues have been delayed because the witnesses got away or the rescuers failed to interview them adequately.

Stop, Think, Plan

Every fiber in your body urges you to hurl yourself after your friends who have just been swept away, find them, dig them out—*you're off to the rescue!* Right? Wrong.

One of the chief reasons we have been so successful as a species is because compassion is hardwired into the human brain. Yet there are times—difficult times—when survival depends on being able to suppress those instincts. Take a step back, calm down, and **stop, think, and plan**. Remember, no one said it would be easy to deal with an avalanche. In an avalanche rescue, your priorities are as follows, listed in order of importance:

1. Yourself
2. The other survivors
3. The victim

First of all, the victim may be just fine and not even need help—or the victim may be mortally injured or already dead. In either case, it makes no sense to risk your life for someone who doesn't need it. Remember that the number-one rule of rescue is to look out for number one—that's you. Stop, think, and plan.

Is It Safe?

Stop and take a minute to add up the facts. If you can't get to the debris safely, don't go. If a loved one is buried under the snow, this will likely be the most difficult decision of your life.

The good news is that most of the time, conditions will be safe, for the same reason that a stick of dynamite is safe after it has already gone off. Most of the time, you can safely descend into the avalanche path or, better yet, come up from the bottom. Whatever you do, don't be tempted to cross an adjacent avalanche path that has not yet slid. Remember, the snowpack just demonstrated to you in no uncertain terms that it's unstable (see Chapter 4, Will It Slide?). If one slope has just avalanched, the identical one next to it will likely do the same if you give it a thump. Choose your route carefully.

When to Consider Saying No

Obviously, it is another very tough call to decide not to attempt a rescue. Numerous times, organized rescue groups have decided to abandon a search because of dangerous or deteriorating conditions—often amid heated debate. But first things first. Look out for number one. Personally, if I could safely access the debris, I might risk doing a quick beacon search, but I would not risk bringing in a larger group of searchers, especially an organized probe line that could take considerable time. Here are some situations in which you might decide not to attempt a rescue:

1. If you're standing above the avalanche and there is too much unslid snow above the crown face ("hangfire") to allow you to safely cross over to get to the crown face (Figure 6-1). I am not aware of any case in which hangfire has come down on its own if it is left undisturbed. Usually you can cross short sections of hangfire safely, say 5 meters (16 feet). However, if the avalanche broke midslope and a disconcerting amount of snow hangs above the fracture, you should try to find a better way onto the debris. This is a tough call.

2. If you're standing below the avalanche, it's almost always safe to travel uphill onto the debris unless you are faced with the following combination of circumstances:
   ❖ Multiple avalanche paths drain onto the rescue area (Figure 6-2).
   ❖ The victim was buried by a spontaneous avalanche that descended from above (rather than it having been human triggered).
   ❖ The weather that caused the avalanche will likely cause more avalanches in the immediate future (heavy loading of new or windblown snow, rain, or rapid melting).

Proceed If It's Safe

If it is safe to go in, then proceed to the next step. As Doug Fesler says, sometimes the best way to go faster is to go slower. Strong emotions, poor communication, equipment problems, and logistical problems all conspire to make rescues

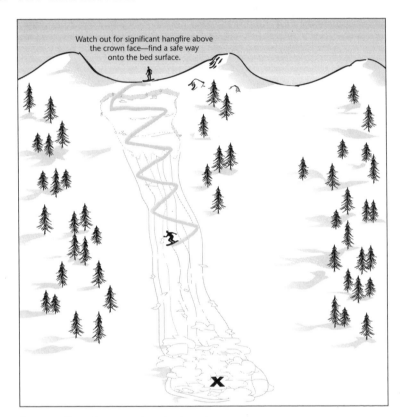

Figure 6-1. Zigzag down or up the avalanche path.

a mess—nearly every rescue, even among professionals. So to reduce the mess factor, *stop, think, and plan.*

❖ Are there any witnesses? Don't let them get away. Ask them for information.

❖ Figure out which group member has the most avalanche rescue experience and appoint that person as the leader.

❖ Take a quick inventory of your equipment—beacons, probes, shovels, first-aid kit.

❖ Find out who's good at what. Put your best beacon people on the job (see Chapter 7, Rescue Techniques).

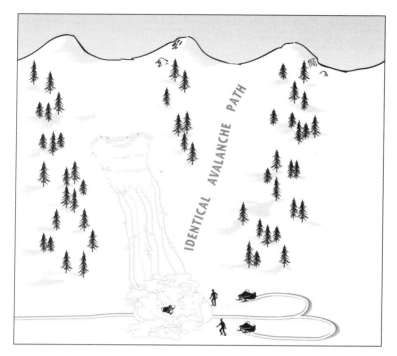

Figure 6-2. Is it safe to do the rescue? When the accident site sits at the bottom of multiple avalanche paths, you have a tough decision to make.

❖ Remind everyone to communicate with the leader.
❖ Remind everyone to keep their equipment with them. Don't litter up the debris. Otherwise, you won't know which equipment belongs to the victim and which belongs to the rescuers.

Now, finally, you are ready to begin a rescue effort.

CHAPTER 7

RESCUE TECHNIQUES

In the Hollywood view of the rescue world, there's drama, action, heroism, a race against time, and heart-pumping action. Injury, death, and rescues capture our imagination. Now that's the way to sell advertising. But the boring truth is that avalanche rescues don't work very well. Rescues even by professionals are usually chaotic and frantic. With the inherent problems of wild emotions, impossible time constraints, lack of resources, nightmarish communication problems, and foul weather, it's a wonder that any avalanche rescues succeed at all.

But we have to be prepared for disaster for two reasons: First, even smart people regularly make mistakes, and second, even without mistakes, the world is a much more random place than we would like to believe. Stuff happens. So my philosophy is that prevention is the best medicine—yet always prepare for the worst.

RESCUE WITH BEACONS

If you and your partners are properly equipped for backcountry sports, you're wearing beacons and know how to use them—right? Which means if the worst happens and someone in your party is caught in an avalanche, you can attempt a rescue using your beacons.

Turn Beacons to "Receive" Mode and Turn Off Mobile Phones

In nearly every avalanche rescue practice I have done with beginning students, someone fails to turn their beacon to the "receive" mode. As a result, the searchers spend the first 10 minutes hopelessly confused by a "mysterious" signal that seems to come and go until they finally trace it to one of their own (we have met the enemy and he is us). Instead, if you hear a signal that doesn't make sense, stop and listen. If the signal changes, that means it's coming from a moving source. In avalanche classes, I don't fight it anymore; I just let the inevitable happen, and it always turns out to be a great learning experience. But if it happens when your friend is buried for real, then you're in deep trouble. (Practice, practice, practice.)

Another common mistake in beacon rescues is that people won't even remember how to turn their beacon to receive. A final common mistake: some beacons automatically return to the "transmit" mode after a few minutes, which is very confusing if, like most people, you read the directions for the first and last time on Christmas Day.

Before you go onto the avalanche debris, the leader should check to make sure that *all beacons are set to receive* and that everyone knows how their beacon works. (See Chapter 8, Rescue Technology, for a detailed discussion on how beacons work.) Mobile phones must be turned off.

Do a Beacon Search

Beacons are "directional," meaning that the receiving beacon gets a stronger signal in one orientation than another—but they are not directional in the way you may think: They don't point directly at the transmitting beacon. Instead, they point along the lines of the transmitting beacon's magnetic field. (As my friend—and engineering PhD—Ian McCammon tells me, it doesn't technically become an "electromagnetic field" until you get farther away than about 100 meters [300 feet] . Whatever.) This magnetic field is an extremely important concept to grasp, so I take some time here to explain it.

Remember back to the science experiments you did in grade school in which you put iron filings on a piece of paper and then put a magnet under the paper. The iron filings lined up along the lines of the magnet's magnetic field. This is a way to visualize the lines of force in two dimensions (the plane of the paper). It's important to realize that the lines of force exist in three dimensions, so they actually look kind of like the shape of an apple. You need to be solid with this concept, so be sure to practice mapping out the curving field with two beacons until you are comfortable with how they work.

Next, there are two common methods for finding buried beacons: the induction method and the grid method. You use the induction method at a distance and the grid method when you get close.

Induction Method

The induction method is also called the "flux line method" or the "tangent method." Simply follow the lines of the magnetic field (aka flux lines) (Figure 7-1) as they lead you on a curving path toward the transmitting beacon—or in a straight line, if you are directly in line with the axis of the buried beacon. Most modern beacons have digital lights or an arrow to show you which way to turn the beacon. With old analog units, you must continually reorient the beacon and listen for the strongest signal. Realize that the beacon will point you in one of two directions,

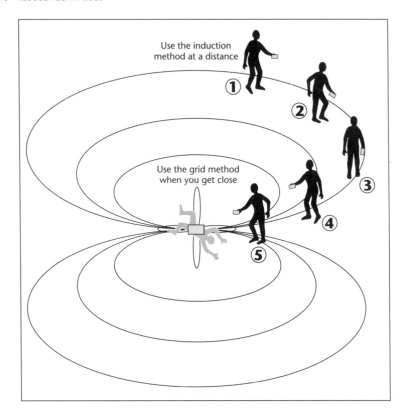

Figure 7-1. The induction method

which are opposite to each other; if the signal gets weaker (the distance numbers go up), you're heading the long way around the semicircle. Turn around and march in the opposite direction. Just follow the beacon's lights or the arrow, which will lead you on a curving path to the transmitting beacon.

Simple. Or at least it's simple in a parking lot. It gets a lot more complicated on a slope, since a curving path sometimes makes you walk uphill (more huffing and puffing just when you need it the least). It can also be complicated on small avalanche paths, where the curving line takes you outside of the avalanche path (possibly dangerous territory) or into a cliff (impenetrable territory). With practice, though, you can figure out ways to get around these problems.

This induction method works well at a distance, but when you get close to the buried beacon, you will need to switch to the grid method, described next.

Grid Method

The grid method works much better at close distances, and most modern beacons automatically switch into the grid mode when you get closer than about 3 meters (9 feet). Start moving in a grid of perpendicular lines, first moving across the slope then up and down the fall line. Make sure you orient the beacon in the same direction and hold it there, like a needle on a compass. At this stage, you don't want to keep turning the beacon, which can give you confusing signals. Where you think the signal is strongest (the lowest distance numbers), you simply make a perpendicular turn (90 degrees to the old direction) and follow this new line. You have two choices of direction. If the signal fades (distance numbers increase), you're going the wrong way, so turn around (180 degrees) and march in the other direction until you hear the strongest signal. Turn 90 degrees again and repeat the process over and over until you zero in on the buried beacon (Figure 7-2).

Figure 7-2. The grid method

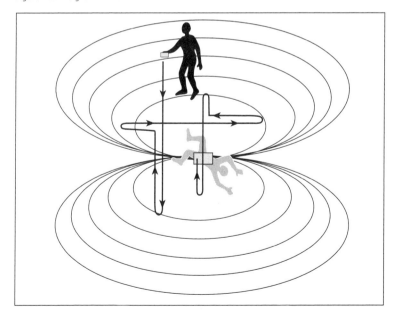

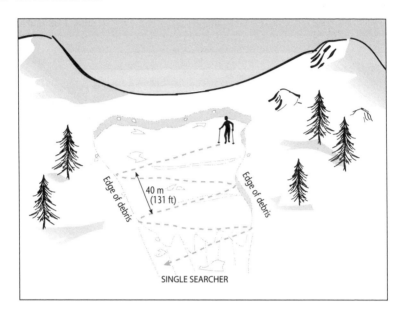

SINGLE SEARCHER

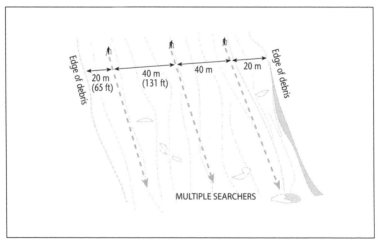

MULTIPLE SEARCHERS

Figures 7-3a and b. Make sure your switchbacks are spaced close enough not to miss a beacon signal (about 40 meters for most beacons but 20 meters for some brands with shorter range).

When you get within a couple of meters (about 6 feet), take off your skis or snowboard. Bend over and run the beacon over the snow surface. Don't alternately stand up and bend over doing the "mating flamingo dance," as Doug Fesler likes to call it. Keep the beacon near the snow all the time and remember to keep it oriented in the same direction.

Start Doing Zigzags and Watch Your Spacing

We do a beacon search similarly to the way we analyze snow and terrain—we start with the large scale, move to the intermediate scale, and then do the fine search. The best way to search a large area with a beacon is to move in a zigzag pattern. This technique is especially effective if you are descending from the top on skis or a snowboard. The length of your zigzags should run from one edge of the avalanche path to the other. Pick a width between your zigzags so that you won't miss a signal (Figure 7-3a and b). The spacing will depend on the minimum range of your particular brand of beacon. For most beacons, the zigzags should be around 40 meters (131 feet). Remember that some beacons have half the range of other beacons, so your spacing with these beacons should be around 20 meters (65 feet).

Note: Especially in maritime climates the bed surface can be very hard and icy, and descending a 35- to 45-degree icy slope can be dangerous. Sometimes people are tempted to descend on the snow that is to the sides of the slide, but this is where you can easily trigger the snow that hasn't yet slid.

Hopefully, you have been regularly practicing with your beacon and you have some intuitive sense for its receiving range. Remember that the buried person's beacon may have weak batteries or be cold or be an old, out-of-date model, in which case, its transmitting range will be less than ideal, which is why we use a distance of 40 meters (131 feet) between zigzags instead of the maximum range of the beacon.

Continually rotate your beacon on all three axes to find the most favorable orientation. The searching beacon receives the strongest signal when its longest antenna is parallel to the lines of the transmitting beacon's magnetic field, but because you don't know the orientation of the buried beacon, you need to continually reorient your beacon until you get the first signal and know what orientation works best for this search.

When You Receive the First Signal

Don't spend a lot of time with the details once you get the first signal. This is the time to move fast and get a *general* idea of where the signal is coming from. If you're using the induction method, don't worry about getting the exact direction. If the signal is

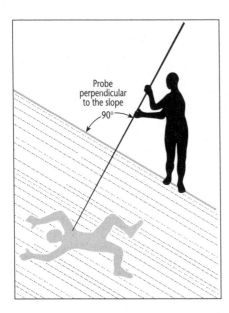

Figure 7-4. Probe perpendicular to the snow surface. Don't worry about injuring the victim with the probe or shovel, which is the least of their worries when they can't breathe.

getting stronger, you're going in the right direction. Keep pointing your beacon in the direction of the arrows on the beacon or the strongest signal (if you are using an old analog beacon), and keep moving. As the Swiss avalanche rescue specialist Manuel Genswein puts it, "It's like an airplane coming in for a landing: go fast when you are far away and go progressively slower the closer you get." At a distance, on foot or snowshoes you should be running or traveling at a fast walk and on skis or a snowboard you should be cruising fast.

When You Get Close

When you get within about 10 meters (33 feet), you need to slow way down. Don't even think about digging yet. Take some time—perhaps 30 seconds—and get the search as exact as possible.

Failing to get an exact location is probably the second most-common mistake among novice beacon searchers (after the first most-common mistake of failing to set their beacon to receive). It's only natural to get excited and shout out, "Here! It's right here!" and then several people whip out their shovels and start flinging snow. After five minutes of furious digging, they still haven't hit anything. Wisely, someone grabs a beacon and takes time to get a more exact location and find that they have been digging a meter (3 feet) away from the victim. Far too many times I have seen overly excited students start digging in the wrong place, sometimes 10 meters (33 feet) away from the victim. Slow down. Get as close as you can (Figure 7-4). Skilled professionals can usually hit the target with a probe on the first try and have a very close guess on the depth.

Probe: After you have zeroed in on the beacon, you still don't start digging yet. First, take out your collapsible probe and get an *exact* location. Start where you think the signal is strongest, probe in an expanding spiral until you hit the victim (Figure 7-5), then leave the probe in place. It takes about 10 seconds to probe an area 2 meters by 2 meters (6 feet by 6 feet) and it takes about 10 minutes to dig a hole that large. Using a probe can locate a victim many times faster than shoveling. Shoveling takes a *huge* amount of time, especially in dense avalanche debris that is often as hard as concrete.

Dig

Digging usually takes more time than searching, so it's essential to practice digging techniques. That's right. Practice digging. I'm not winning many friends here, but it's important to talk about the very loathsome topic of digging techniques.

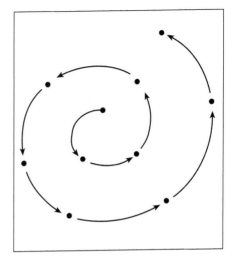

Figure 7-5. When you locate the strongest signal, probe in an expanding spiral until you get a strike. Leave the probe in place and start digging downhill from the probe.

Don't Dig the Wrong Way

Most people dig completely wrong. They stand on top of the victim, dig straight down, and make the hole far too small: all wrong. First, buried victims have a hard time breathing because the snow presses on their rib cage and diaphragm, making it hard to expand their lungs. Rescuers standing on top of the victim while they dig further exacerbate the problem. For this reason, you start digging *downhill* of the victim and dig toward them horizontally.

Also, it is always much easier to move snow horizontally out of a hole than to lift it vertically. Third, you need a much larger hole than you might imagine because you will likely need room to work on the victim. Often you must completely extricate victims and turn them over to begin CPR.

Dig the Right Way

Leave the probe in place. Start digging from the *downhill* side of the victim and dig horizontally toward them. With several diggers, make like a flock of geese and dig in a V shape so each person can chip away at the side walls and pass the snow

Figure 7-6. Shoveling technique is even more important than beacon technique because it takes more time. Recent research from Europe indicates that shovelers should make like a flock of geese and form a V on the downhill side of the probe (victim). Move the debris out of the middle of the V. Move snow horizontally instead of trying to lift it out of the hole. Rotate positions every couple of minutes. (From Manuel Genswein, "Easy Searcher")

out into the middle (Figure 7-6). The V should be about twice as long as it is deep. The person digging at the point of the V will do the most work, so it's important to rotate diggers every two minutes, the same way bicycle racers take their turn in the lead, then rotate to the back of the pack to recover. Pass the debris down the middle of the V. Don't lift the snow, but instead slide it sideways, which takes much less effort.

Searching for Multiple Victims

Even though the chance of actually having to perform a multiple beacon search is small, we still need to practice multiple search techniques for the small percentage of the time when we may need it. Unless we have been regularly practicing with multiple beacon problems, pulling off such a rescue in a realistic situation will likely be an insurmountable problem. Again, practice, practice, practice.

When using beacons with analog sound, you will easily hear if there is more than one beacon transmitting. It will sound like a staggered *beep-beep…beep-beep*.

Since beacons usually transmit at different rates, you can hear the interaction of the cadence overlap as it changes through time as well. With practice, you will be able to tell how many beacons are transmitting and also concentrate on the strongest signal while tuning out the others the same way you can follow one person's conversation at a crowded dinner table.

Most brands of digital beacons produce a sound that is digitally produced so that it locks onto the strongest signal and suppresses the sound from other beacons, which helps locate a single beacon faster. But for multiple beacons, you will have to practice with more sophisticated techniques. Most digital beacons have a lockout feature, which "flags" or locks out the signal from the beacon that you just found so that you can hear the signal from the next closest beacon. The lockout feature works fairly well, but perhaps 10–20 percent of the time it fails to work

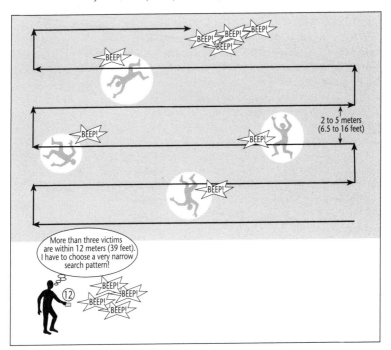

Figure 7-7. The micro search is one effective method for multiple burials. Even with beacons that have a "lockout" feature, you should practice this technique because the lockout will not work some of the time due to signal overlap. (From Manuel Genswein, "Easy Searcher")

(because the cadence of the two signals happen to be in phase with each other). In this case, you have to use a method like the one below. The multiple search strategies are slightly different for each brand of beacon, so be sure to follow the directions from the beacon manufacturer and, again, practice a lot.

When the Lockout Feature Does Not Work.

When the lockout feature on your beacon does not seem to work, you can use either the micro strip search (as shown in Figure 7-7) or use the expanding circles method, in which you walk a 5-meter (16-foot) circle around the last beacon found to try and pick up another signal, then expand the circle to 10 meters, then 20 meters, etc. Either method works well.

Performing Triage for Multiple Victims

Unfortunately, with multiple burials we sometimes have to make some hard choices. In the backcountry, most of the time we have limited resources and we need to evaluate which victims are most likely to live and search for them first.

Look for the shallow burials in open areas first. After you get all the shallowly buried victims breathing and uncover their chest so they can expand their lungs, then go back and search for the deeply buried ones. Deep burials, say 1.5 meters (5 feet) or more deep, have a very small chance of survival. How fast can you dig a 5-foot-deep hole in dense avalanche debris? The numbers usually don't add up to a happy ending.

A scenario like this takes a lot of discipline and hard choices are required. Wasting valuable time digging out a victim in a deep burial doesn't make sense when you may be able to get a victim out of a shallow burial much more quickly.

Also, ignore the person on the surface who is screaming in pain or fear. We're worried about the ones who can't scream because they can't even breathe. Deal with the screamers later. The exception to this is if the person on the surface is losing blood rapidly or has some other condition that requires immediate attention. Quickly stop the bleeding and return to the task of getting everyone breathing.

Provide First Aid

I strongly recommend that anyone who regularly travels in the backcountry take at least a basic first-aid course. All serious backcountry travelers should have a wilderness first-responder certification or equivalent. (See Resources.) This is an avalanche book, not a first-aid book, but I'll cover some basics.

Here's the mantra: ABCDE—airway, breathing, circulation, disability, environment. Here's how to put it into practice:

A: Airway. Do all the rescued people have unobstructed airways? Remove snow from mouths and noses if necessary.

B: Breathing. Are all the rescued people breathing? If not, perform CPR unless contraindicated as with massive trauma.

C: Circulation. Stop the bleeding.

D: Disability. Most avalanche victims will have some sort of traumatic injury so you may have to stabilize the spine or splint major fractures.

E: Environment. Get the victim out of the snow and keep him or her warm. Don't forget to insulate underneath them; preferably use a foam pad or synthetic insulation.

In recent years, most people carry a cell phone, and probably as a result, it seems that fewer people carry an adequate first-aid kit and extra warm clothes. Don't fall for this trap. Helicopters can't fly in poor weather or after nightfall, and even when they can fly, often they can't land or long-line emergency personnel into complex, steep terrain. At a minimum, you should always carry a basic first-aid kit, extra hat and mittens, a down or synthetic-fill jacket, a lightweight bivy bag (lightweight space blanket or garbage bag at a minimum). Puff pants are also a good idea, especially in more remote areas. See the 9th Commandment in Chapter 5, Low-Risk Travel Ritual.

Go for Help

Yes, now—finally—is the time to go for help if you don't have communication, such as a cell phone connection or a personal locator. Aren't you glad that you didn't send someone for help earlier? First things first. You need all your resources at the scene to get everyone dug out and breathing as soon as possible. Now you can take the time to plan how someone is going to go for help without getting killed. Now you have the time to write down all the accident details so that you can communicate to the rescuers three pieces of essential information:

1. the exact location of the avalanche
2. the best route for the rescuers to access the area
3. exactly what kind of injuries the victims have

Many people who frantically call for help early in a rescue don't know any of these details, which are essential information for a rescue team—especially the exact location. Countless hours have been wasted because of this, not to mention rescuers' lives being put at risk. Remember it's good to place a cell phone call early in the rescue to notify rescuers that you *might* need their help, but this phone call shouldn't be made at the expense of doing the rescue yourself quickly and efficiently.

RESCUE WITHOUT BEACONS

The only thing worse than doing an avalanche rescue is doing one without beacons. As Dale Atkins says, it's like looking for a needle in a haystack by using a needle. Not surprisingly, very few victims who are completely buried without a beacon will survive. Beacons are very inexpensive when compared to a human life, especially your own. Even if beacons fail to save a life, they do save your friends from having to spend all night probing for you.

Rescue without a beacon means using a probe. Everyone in your group should have either collapsible probe poles or avalanche probe ski poles; if not, then you will have to go all the way back to the Stone Age and use tree branches or whatever else you can find.

Do an Initial Search

Some people also refer to the initial probe search as a "hasty search," but I don't like that term because it implies that speed is more important than thoroughness. In what is more commonly called an "initial search" or a "scuff search," in a beaconless search, move quickly down or up the avalanche path and concentrate on places where the avalanche has piled up snow, such as:

❖ debris piled on the uphill side of trees
❖ debris collected on the outside of turns or benches
❖ debris at the bottom of the avalanche path

Also concentrate on areas around clues, such as:

❖ a ski or ski pole
❖ a glove or hat
❖ a snowmobile

In each one of these areas (Figure 7-8), do the following:

1. Look carefully for anything sticking out of the snow—a hand, a glove, or a ski—and follow it to see if the victim is attached. Probe around these areas. Too many tragic deaths have occurred because the victim's partners noticed a ski or a snowmobile on the surface but did not check the evidence out further. Note: Because they are larger, snowmobiles often end up on the surface and their riders end up buried less than 1 meter (2 to 3 feet) deep and 3 to 10 meters (10 to 40 feet) uphill of and in line with the snowmobile.
2. Spot probe these likely areas by random probing. Don't spend a lot of time probing at this stage. Try to cover the entire avalanche path in about 10 to 15 minutes.
3. Occasionally shout and listen for the victim's response. Some people have been found this way. Also, although the snow absorbs most of the sound

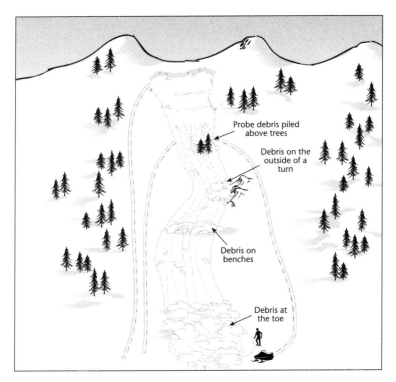

Figure 7-8. Concentrate your initial search on places where avalanche debris has piled up.

coming out of the snow, the victim can usually hear sound filtering into the snow from outside.

Organize Your Probing

If the initial search turns up nothing, then your victim(s) are most likely completely buried. Don't send someone away from the scene to get help, at least not yet. You need all your resources to search. If you have no luck after about an hour, then send someone to get help.

Again, if you have cell phone, radio, or personal locator beacon coverage, then go ahead and call for help right away rather than sending someone, because you will likely need that someone to help on site.

If you have only a couple of searchers, it's probably best to continue to do spot probing of likely areas. If you have, say, four or more people, then organize them into probe lines, but only after doing a complete initial search of the debris.

For a probe line, start in the most likely area—for instance, in line with a clue (ski, snowmobile, glove, etc.) or downhill from the last-seen area. *Start at the bottom* of the avalanche debris and work your way uphill.

Especially for small groups of searchers, the three-hole probe has the highest probability of finding someone. Line up across the slope with arms outstretched, each person spaced wrist to wrist from the searchers on either side. Then each searcher probes three times, once to the left, once in the center, and once to the right, keeping the holes about 50 centimeters (1.6 feet) apart (Figure 7-9). Keep track of the probe holes in order to keep the probes evenly spaced, and watch to make sure everyone stays in a straight line. Organized probing is much easier if one person can take the lead and call out the signals: "Probe right. Probe center. Probe left. Step forward."

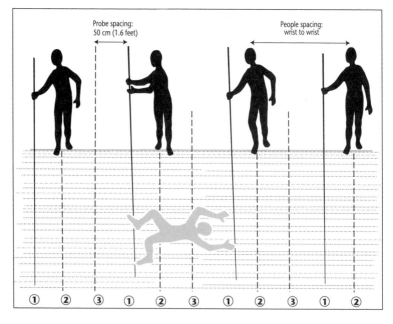

Figure 7-9. Searchers line up wrist to wrist. Probe once left, once center, once right, and then move forward one step.

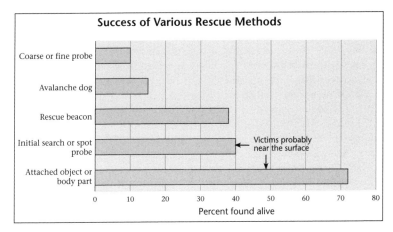

Figure 7-10. The success of these various rescue methods is a function of how fast the victim was rescued and how deeply they were buried. Most victims found by attached body part or hasty search were probably at or near the surface and found quickly by partners. Avalanche dog and coarse probing are usually done by organized rescue teams, which often take several hours to get to the accident site. (From Dale Atkins)

This kind of "coarse probing" has about an 80 percent chance of finding a victim on the first pass. Statistically, this is the most efficient use of resources because of its combination of speed and thoroughness. Probe all the likely areas. If you have reason to think that you may have missed a victim on one pass, make another pass.

If there are multiple victims, and/or you successfully uncover any victims, see the triage and first-aid sections in Rescue with Beacons, above.

Go for Help

If you have not had any success after about an hour, then it's time to send someone for help. An organized rescue team will come in with search dogs; if the dogs can't locate the victim, then the searchers will form larger teams of probers to perform a fine probe of the entire area (Figure 7-10).

If they have no success with probes and dogs—which is common with very deep burials—they may have no choice but to leave the victim to melt out in spring. And yes, the price of a beacon is always better than putting loved ones through that.

DEALING WITH THE AFTERMATH

The death of a friend or loved one is one of the most difficult events most of us have to face in our lives, and I have, unfortunately, faced it several times. Luckily, we don't have to do it alone. Don't try to be a tough guy and shove it back in some hidden place or dissipate the pain through work, alcohol, drugs, or fooling around. I've seen post-traumatic stress syndrome significantly disrupt the lives of several of my colleagues, as well as myself. So take it from me. Get some professional help. That's what it's for.

Even if there is no death, perhaps you just took a very scary ride in an avalanche and suddenly came face to face with your own mortality. This is often a life-changing event. You have to expect it to take some time before the echoes quit reverberating off the canyon walls of your psyche. It takes time and work. Don't cheat yourself.

TAKE-HOME POINT

Avalanche rescues—even by professionals—don't work very well. The best avalanche rescue is to never need one. But we are all human, after all, which means we make mistakes. Occasionally, we will need to do a rescue, so we need to practice regularly in realistic situations. Practice, practice, practice.

CHAPTER 8

RESCUE TECHNOLOGY

It's our birthright as Americans to always look for the perfect technology so that we don't have to think anymore. Rescue technology has made great strides, especially in the past 15 years, and many people have been saved because of it. So it's important to know how the new rescue tools work.

But, as history has repeatedly shown, better rescue technology saves fewer lives than we would expect. That's because we humans tend to practice "risk homeostasis." As conditions (or technology) make things safer, we raise our level of risk to match our preferred comfort level. We take more risks. (See Chapter 1, How Dangerous Is the Brain?) Rescue technology has not replaced, nor probably ever will replace, avalanche avoidance. The best rescue technology is to never need a rescue in the first place.

But our gizmos, used properly, definitely save lives. If we look at automobiles, the fatality rate per million miles driven is only one-third as high now as it was in 1980 before laws on mandatory seat belts and vehicle air bags were passed (from 3.4 to 1.1 deaths per 100 million vehicle miles driven). Seat belts and air bags have not decreased accidents, but they have significantly decreased fatalities. I hope we can achieve similar reductions in avalanche deaths by using avalanche rescue technology.

AVALANCHE BEACONS

I hate to admit that I am old enough to have been recreating in the backcountry when beacons first arrived on the scene back in the 1970s. (Before this, we used avalanche cords, which we dragged behind us.) We all assumed then that beacons would dramatically reduce avalanche deaths, yet the opposite occurred. What happened?

First, better equipment combined with large population booms in the western states led to more and more people recreating in avalanche terrain. And second, because of the aforementioned risk homeostasis (gizmo madness), beacons tend to give us a false sense of security, which not only causes us to jump onto slopes we would normally avoid, but encourages even more people to recreate in avalanche terrain, making it somewhat of a self-perpetuating system.

Beacons give us a false sense of security because the sad truth is that although beacons work well, the people who use them don't always work so well. Many studies have shown that at least among recreational users who do not practice enough, the use of beacons reduces mortality, but only by about 11 percent (some studies have shown 0 percent). More recent studies with the new generation of digital beacons have pushed that number up to 15 to 60 percent, depending on how much practice you do with your beacon and terrain choices.

During my first year on the Bridger Bowl Ski Patrol in Montana back in 1977, we discovered that although beacons seem like simple devices, even professional patrollers flail when doing beacon searches in realistic situations. So we instituted weekly practice sessions. Because of regular practice by professionals in the United States, today the use of beacons reduces mortality by 60 percent. In Switzerland, where people are highly avalanche-educated, the reduction in mortality even among general users is similar. Yet the vast majority of recreational users in the United States rarely practice, and when they do, it is seldom in realistic scenarios. As a result, beacons give a false sense of security and have not reduced avalanche deaths nearly as much as we had hoped.

The good news on beacons: Despite a huge amount of research and money thrown at other ways of finding an avalanche victim, locating a victim through the use of electronic avalanche rescue beacons remains the most widely used way to find someone completely buried in avalanche debris. With regular practice in realistic situations, you should be able to find a buried beacon in under 10 minutes. Among people who practice regularly, beacons may save half of completely buried victims. Beacons will never save everyone because one out of four are killed by trauma; about the same number are buried too deeply to be dug out in time, or they are buried in such a large avalanche path that the rescuers can't get to them in time. Beacons are not silver bullets.

TAKE HOME POINT

Beacons have the potential to save up to half of those who otherwise would have been killed, but only if users practice often in realistic situations. This also means that half of those wearing beacons will die anyway, so we must also behave as if we are not wearing one—in other words, take no extra risks.

Beacon Technology

Avalanche beacons, sometimes called transceivers, are electronic devices the size of a double pack of playing cards, costing $150–$500, that both transmit and receive an electronic signal. (Avalanche beacons are not to be confused with personal locator beacons, which use satellite GPS technology.) Everyone in the party wears a beacon, and each member turns it on before they head into the backcountry. (Wear it *under* your jacket to keep the batteries warm and to keep it from being torn from your body during an avalanche ride.) When turned on, the beacon automatically starts transmitting, about one electronic *"beep"* per second. If someone is buried, everyone else in the party turns their beacons to receive, so that they can hear the beeping of the buried victim's beacon; the signal gets stronger the closer you get (see Rescue with Beacons in Chapter 7, Rescue Techniques). The range of most beacons is 60 to 80 meters (and about that many yards), or about half that range for some makes and models.

This book would be twice as thick if I discussed the technology behind the various brands of beacons and the pros and cons of each. And even if I did, the technology changes so fast that by the time you read this, it would be out of date. (I recommend www.beaconreviews.com as a good place to start researching beacons.) As to which is the best brand, they all work well and there are pros and cons to each. In both formal and informal polls among professional avalanche forecasters about which beacons they use, the results are scattered all over the map, and when there are competitions on how fast people can find hidden beacons, no one brand stands out. The best beacon is the one your partner practices with.

If you have an old analog beacon, you should definitely replace it. The modern digital beacons with multiple antennas are much faster, reduce confusion, and offer more sophisticated features for multiple burial situations. Plus, in many of the older beacons the radio frequency tends to drift as they age, so many of these beacons can't be detected by modern beacons until you get close. Toss the old one and whip out your wallet.

Know How to Use Your Beacon

I can't count the number of times that my supposedly competent friends have forgotten how to turn their beacons to receive or forgotten that they have it programmed to return to transmit after five minutes. How are you going to know whether you can even use your beacon unless you practice? Practice may be a pain, but it sure beats finding out during an avalanche rescue that you don't know your beacon's settings or how to change them.

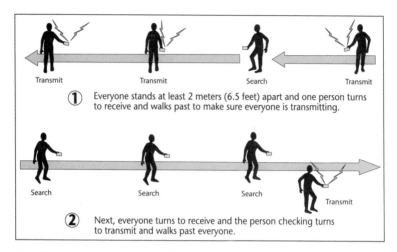

Figure 8-1. Always do a beacon check at the beginning of every tour. Otherwise, you have no way of knowing when someone's beacon is not working or is defective. Also, it reminds everyone how to use the basic features of their beacon. (From Manuel Genswein, "Easy Searcher")

Always Do a Beacon Check at the Beginning of a Tour

I always do a beacon check before everyone heads into the backcountry. Perhaps dozens of times, I have found that someone's beacon—and sometimes my own beacon—just didn't work or it had a compromised transmit or receive range or had weak or corroded batteries. (I always carry a spare in my car because it happens so often.) Before you head out, make sure your beacon is working.

The person doing the check should stand well away from the others, turn his or her beacon to receive, and listen for each person's signal as they travel past (Figure 8-1). This way, you can check the transmit range of each beacon. (Transmit range goes down, often dramatically, on an aging or defective beacon.) Finally, someone else in the group should check the checker in the same way.

Always Practice with Beacons

Another reason to practice: it's better than finding out during a real rescue that you were just not practiced enough to save your friend or spouse.

At home: Do a shell game. If there's no snow in your backyard, take a bunch of grocery bags out of the recycle bin and head outside. Turn a beacon on, hide it in one of the grocery bags, and scatter the other empty grocery bags on the lawn.

Put a rock in each one if the wind is blowing. (Windy conditions are your first clue that beacon practice rather than a tour might be a good idea today.) Then tell your partner to find the beacon. Now switch roles.

If you have more than two beacons, "bury" two of them to do a multiple beacon practice, which is much harder. Then head to the local park where you can practice using the full range of the beacons.

In the field: While you're waiting for someone to run a car shuttle or unload snow-mobiles or perhaps during lunch, put a transmitting beacon into your spare mitten (to protect it from cold and snow). *Make sure it's transmitting.* Stuff the mitten-covered beacon into the snow, the deeper the better. Make some tracks around the area so your partners can't use visual clues, then have them search for the beacon.

Once you are accomplished at finding beacons next to the snowy parking lot, move onto steeper slopes. After you master that, move up to multiple burials and then graduate to finding multiple burials in realistic situations: on slopes, in jumbled avalanche debris, in deeper burials. Add several rescuers looking at once so you have the usual cluster of communication and logistics problems.

Then, finally, add a frantic or uncooperative witness or two, and do it during a blizzard. You will quickly discover that your beacon skills are not nearly as good as you thought. For multiple burials, practice using one of the micro search methods described in Chapter 7. Remember, practice with multiple burials, or your beacon training is not complete.

SHOVELS

Probably the only item more important than a beacon is a shovel, because digging someone out of avalanche debris without one is nearly impossible. I like the lightweight, heat-tempered aluminum shovels that disassemble into two pieces for easy storage in any pack. Get the ones with the D-shaped grip and the extendable handle. You can buy them in most outdoor shops. Avoid cheap plastic shovels because they break more often, and they don't seem to chop through ice chunks and tree branches as well—and, yes, many avalanche debris piles are mixed with tree branches.

Snowmobilers: Be sure to wear your shovel and probe in a small pack on your back instead of carrying them on the machine. If your snowmobile gets buried with your shovel on it, you won't be able to dig anyone else out who might also be buried.

AVALANCHE PROBES

I carry a collapsible avalanche probe in my pack all the time. Even when I carry my probe ski poles, I still carry the collapsible probe pole in my pack. Why? Because out of the hundreds of students I have taught through the years, I have almost never seen anyone who could assemble their ski pole probes in under 10 minutes. It takes a while to remember how they work, then it takes a long time to get the baskets off. By that time the folks with the collapsible probes have already been probing for several minutes. And remember how long the buried victim has before asphyxiation? Maybe 15 minutes.

Collapsible probes assemble quickly, they're longer, and they slide through the snow much more easily than ski pole probes do. Finally, they are lightweight; I don't even notice one in my pack. Many pros strap a collapsible probe to their shovel handle along with flagging for marking clues, the route to the avalanche accident, and the perimeter of the avalanche debris.

AVALANCHE AIR BAGS

An avalanche air bag (sometimes called an avalanche balloon pack) is the avalanche equivalent of a life jacket. Technically, they don't "float" you to the surface of the snow as life jackets float you in water, but in the granular flow of an avalanche, larger objects rise to the surface, and the air bag once inflated makes you bigger. If you are caught in an avalanche, you pull the handle on your pack strap and the air bag(s) quickly inflate (using either a compressed air cartridge or a battery-powered fan), which will quickly "float" you to the surface. (Big-wave surfers are now using a similar approach with cartridge-inflated wet suits.) Avalanche air bags work because the two most time-consuming parts of a rescue are searching and digging; and if the victim ends up on the surface—no searching, no digging.

There has been some controversy and confusion over their effectiveness. In a major, peer-reviewed study by Haegeli et al., in 2014, they found that in accidents, an inflated avalanche air bag saved the lives of half of the victims who would have otherwise have died. They also found that in 20 percent of the cases, the victims did not or could not inflate the avalanche air bag, so accounting for noninflations, air bags saved 41 percent of those who would have otherwise died. But you sometimes see another statistic used in advertisements, like the one sitting here on my desk, that they have a "97 percent success rate in real-world use"—which is only half true. What you often don't hear is the other half of the statistic—that there's an 81 percent "success rate" even without using an air bag. In this case, they are talking about people caught instead of about just those who would have otherwise been killed. This is an important distinction because avalanches are surprisingly benevolent, and many of the people caught will survive anyway. They are either able to escape off the slab, the avalanche is small, they self-arrest on the bed surface, they are saved by beacons, or they just plain get lucky. The "97 percent

Avalanche air bags are inflated by pulling a rip cord if you are caught in avalanche. They can "float" you to the surface of moving avalanche debris.

success rate" statistic includes the 80 to 90 percent of those caught who would have survived anyway.

Most of us are probably more interested in how many people would be saved by the technology. Thus, I usually repeat the aforementioned study that avalanche air bags will save a little less than half of those who would have otherwise died. An avalanche air bag can never save all people because of those killed, one out of four dies from the trauma of hitting trees and rocks on the way down. An additional one out of four dies from deep burial in a terrain trap or from being caught at the bottom of a slope where the avalanche does not travel far enough for the "floating" process of inverse segregation to work. In these cases, neither beacons nor air bags will make much difference. We also have to remember that about 20 percent will not be able to pull the air bag trigger in time. That said, avalanche air bags have become an important new technology, and they are rapidly becoming standard equipment for most avalanche professionals and serious backcountry travelers.

AVALUNG

People buried under snow die quickly from rebreathing their own exhaled carbon dioxide; an Avalung greatly delays this process. The Avalung is simply a lightweight tube worn over the outside of your jacket or attached to a pack. If you get caught in an avalanche, you push the plastic mouthpiece toward your mouth—kept properly positioned in case of such an occurrence—and start breathing through it. The tube allows you to breathe in through the intake near your chest (thus filtering out the snow that normally plugs up your throat). When you breathe out, a flapper valve directs your air out through the end of the tube, which is near your side or back, keeping the carbon dioxide well away from the intake.

In tests, buried volunteers have been able to breathe under the snow for over an hour with no ill effects. Because this device was introduced relatively recently, there are not enough statistics to show its effectiveness. But as of this writing, there have been over a dozen incidents in which the buried victim used an Avalung, and in several of these incidents, out of multiple people buried, the ones using the Avalung survived while their companions without Avalungs died.

The obvious question with the Avalung is whether you will be able to chomp down on the mouthpiece in the first few seconds after you are caught in an avalanche; you won't be able to do it while you're getting thrashed around during the ride.

However, the prognosis seems good. The mouthpiece is stiff enough that you can position it near your mouth when you need it. Also, it's apparently tough enough to withstand the forces inside most avalanches. Although there are exceptions, it appears that most of the victims to date did not have trouble getting it in their mouth and keeping it there on the descent.

The bottom line is that the Avalung is light and cheap, and there are few excuses not to wear one. I use a pack that has an Avalung manufactured into the pack strap, so I always have it with me. Since many recreational users just don't practice their beacon, probing, and digging skills often enough, an Avalung can buy you time until your friend can dig you out. That's why I use an Avalung. The exception is when I wear an avalanche air bag pack, because it's too hard to both pull the trigger for that and get the Avalung in my mouth.

RECCO

RECCO is a rescue system in which people wear small, inexpensive chips (or reflectors) manufactured into many popular brands of helmets, clothing, and boots. The reflectors don't emit a signal or use batteries; they're passive. The reflector is simply an antenna attached to a diode that doubles the frequency of and reflects back the broadcast signal from the searching unit (called a detector) used by organized rescue teams. The directional signal allows the operator to quickly locate a buried victim.

As a search tool for organized rescue teams (ski patrols and mountain rescue) the RECCO system does not replace an avalanche transceiver, the best device for companion rescue. Originally developed for use inside ski areas, where customers don't normally wear transceivers, the RECCO system has been found to be useful in-bounds, out-of-bounds, and even far into the backcountry. Almost all avalanche-prone ski areas and many mountain rescue teams throughout the world have RECCO detectors ready to be quickly dispatched. The RECCO system gives organized teams another method and another chance to find people. The downside is that rescuers must be notified and respond. The upside is that once on site, they have an electronic device to search large areas quickly. So far no live recoveries have occurred in the backcountry of North America using RECCO, though there have been a number of body recoveries. However, there have been several live recoveries every winter in Europe, and as rescue times become faster and faster in North America, we will likely see more live recoveries using RECCO.

Although an avalanche air bag or a transceiver and a skilled partner still provide the best chance for a live recovery, it's cheap insurance to buy clothing or gear with RECCO reflectors.

THE PERFECTLY EQUIPPED AVALANCHE GEEK

So what does all this mean? As usual, our choice of terrain almost always makes more difference than the rescue gear we carry. If you choose low-consequence terrain and travel with skilled partners, then rescue gear can probably save a life in most avalanche involvements. If you choose high-consequence terrain, then all the avalanche rescue gear in the world will make almost no difference.

Remember that even if we perform a textbook rescue, one out of four people will die from trauma of hitting trees and rocks during the avalanche and an additional one out of four will end up deeply buried in a terrain trap or deeply buried by a secondary avalanche. With an avalanche air bag, they may be caught in a short-duration avalanche with not enough time for the inverse segregation process to work, or victims will not trigger the air bag in time.

By now your head is probably swimming—beacon, shovel, probe, avalanche air bag, Avalung, RECCO—how much of this stuff do you really need? And what does it cost and weigh? Where to draw the line?

My minimum kit includes a beacon, a shovel, a probe, an Avalung, and a RECCO. They are all lightweight and, with the exception of the beacon, are cheap. The avalanche air bag pack is the heaviest and most expensive, but it's also the technology that probably has the best chance of saving my life. So there's the tradeoff. As air bag packs get lighter and cheaper, they will undoubtedly become ubiquitous, perhaps required, equipment, like wearing a PFD on a white-water river.

This is the minimum avalanche gear I carry with me at all times—beacon, shovel, probe, and Avalung. Notice I have two beacons in case someone else's beacon does not work. I sometimes leave the spare beacon in the car after we do a beacon check at the trailhead, and I sometimes bring it with me to do a beacon practice during lunch.

Good News—Bad News

The good news is that these gizmos can help to save lives. The bad news is that they probably won't save nearly as many as we hope. It's basic human nature to adjust our level of acceptable risk upward with each "revolutionary" safety device that we use. Seat belts, automobile air bags, and safer highway engineering have decreased automobile deaths but not accidents, because we all just drive that much farther, faster, and crazier. (More on this in Chapter 1, How Dangerous Is the Brain?)

Yes, some people will be saved who would otherwise have died, but nearly as many will likely die because the technology gives them the confidence to venture into progressively more extreme activities. It's no wonder that of people wearing beacons or inflated air bags, as many are recovered dead as those who are found alive. Greater safety also allows for greater utility (powder and fun), so people will expose themselves to avalanche hazard more and the fatality rate will not decrease as much as we hope.

Finally, the success of avalanche rescue technology depends critically on our choice of terrain and using safe travel rituals. If we choose low-consequence terrain with a small chance of trauma and deep burials in terrain traps, plus travel one at a time with trusted partners, then avalanche rescue gear has a good chance of making a difference in the outcome of a burial. On the other hand, if we choose zero-tolerance-for-error terrain, then rescue gear will make zero difference. Rescue gear is like paying our insurance bills; we do it, but we hope we never have to use that insurance.

CHAPTER 9

PUTTING IT ALL TOGETHER

In this chapter, we put everything together. First, I explain how three factors—hazard, exposure, and vulnerability—combine to determine risk level. Then, I describe a typical day when I go on a backcountry tour, including the step-by-step sequence of how I gather information and make decisions.

THE RISK EQUATION

I promise this is the only equation in this book—and it doesn't even involve any math. Risk to a person in an avalanche depends on (1) hazard, (2) exposure to the hazard, and (3) vulnerability (Figure 9-1). That's it. Let me explain the different parts:

Hazard

Hazard is the thing that can cause harm to a person exposed to it. In this case, the hazard comes from an avalanche, which, in 93 percent of cases, we ourselves trigger. This is good because it means we can control most of our exposure to the hazard.

As we saw in Chapter 4, hazard has two components: probability and consequences. Probability means the likelihood of an avalanche occurring. Consequences mean what will happen if an avalanche occurs.

To explain all this, I like to use the example of Russian roulette. If we have a six-shooter, probability is determined by the number of bullets loaded into the chambers: one bullet means a likelihood of one out of six, two bullets mean a likelihood of two out of six (or one out of three), and so on. The consequences are determined by what kind of bullet the pistol shoots. For instance, ranging from low consequence to high consequence, the pistol could shoot a blank, a spit wad, a wax bullet, a 22 round, or a 44 magnum.

In other words, the same hazard can be created by combining low probability with high consequences, high probability with low consequences, or an equal

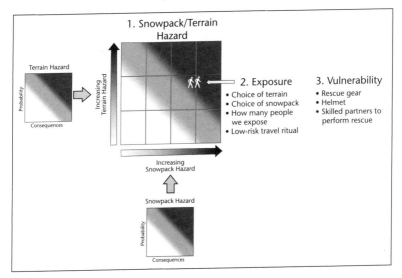

Figure 9-1. Risk is a function of hazard, exposure, and vulnerability. Hazard is danger, something that can cause potential harm—in this case, an avalanche. It's useful to separate this into the hazard of the snowpack and the hazard of the terrain. Both have components of probability (likelihood of triggering) and consequences (size of the avalanche or bad consequences of terrain such as trees, cliffs, terrain traps, etc.). Exposure is people exposed to the hazard. We limit our exposure through our choice of terrain and choice of snowpack. We can often further mitigate our exposure through low-risk travel ritual (one at a time, escape routes, etc.). Vulnerability is how at-risk we are if we are involved in an avalanche, which we can mitigate by carrying personal protection equipment and having skilled partners who can perform a rescue.

mixture of both. Of course, high probability combined with high consequences always means high hazard.

If you're not very familiar with graphs, it's worth staring at Figure 4-4 for a while until it makes sense. It is the only way I know to graphically explain the infinite number of ways to combine the two factors to determine the level of danger.

I also like to separate the hazard of the snowpack and the hazard of the terrain. In the case of terrain, the probability of triggering an avalanche is determined by steepness. The closer it is to 39 degrees, the more likely we are to trigger an avalanche. The consequences related to terrain are determined by what happens if we trigger an avalanche. Do we go into trees, cliffs, or a terrain trap? The snowpack

Photo 9-1. Yes, this is boring terrain, but it's where most people go when an avalanche warning is in effect. It's surprising how fun 25-to-30-degree slopes can be. On a snowmobile, you can have fun playing all day in a flat meadow.

hazard comes from the likelihood of triggering an avalanche (probability) and the size of the avalanche (consequences).

Exposure

We manage our exposure to avalanche hazard through our terrain choices and low-risk travel practices. For instance, with a very hazardous snowpack, we would simply avoid avalanche terrain: Stay on gentle slopes not locally connected to steep ones (Photo 9-1). No exposure—no risk. Or, if we want to get into steep terrain, we have to choose a safer snowpack. With a hazard we think is manageable, we can control our exposure to it by using low-risk travel rituals. In other words, we control our risk mainly by managing our exposure to the hazard.

Vulnerability

Vulnerability means how susceptible we are to being killed or injured if we are caught in an avalanche. For instance, you are much less vulnerable to an avalanche when you are inside a building or on a bus than when you are out in the open on the snow. Similarly, if we wear good rescue equipment, know how to use it, and travel with skilled partners, we are also less vulnerable to the hazard. A helmet makes us less vulnerable to trauma on the way down if we hit trees or rocks. Performing a slope cut or being belayed by a rope will make us less vulnerable to a triggered avalanche.

A Risk-Evaluation Scenario

As we have seen in the rest of this book, we manage our own risk by tweaking different parts of the risk equation. We do this mainly by managing our exposure to the hazard through terrain choices and practicing low-risk travel rituals.

The central hazard diagram of snowpack versus terrain is the main focus of this book, so spend some time studying Figure 9-2 until it's intuitive. The key is to continually manage the combination of terrain hazard and snowpack hazard to keep you in the Low Danger part of the diagram.

The combination of terrain and snowpack is critically important: Most avalanche incidents occur because we don't match the hazard of the snowpack with an appropriate hazard of terrain. If you combine hazardous snowpack with hazardous terrain, you're in trouble. You have to combine dangerous snowpack with safe

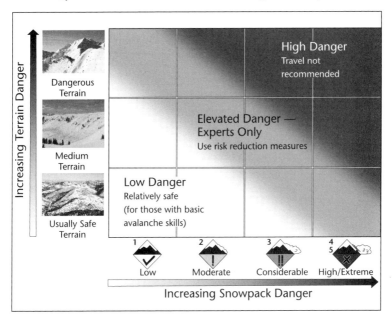

Figure 9-2. Avalanche danger depends on the interaction between snowpack and terrain. We must adjust our terrain choices based on the snowpack. Notice we can safely mix dangerous terrain with a safe snowpack—or safe terrain with a dangerous snowpack—but you can never combine a dangerous snowpack with dangerous terrain. Most avalanche accidents occur in the High Danger and the Elevated Danger–Experts Only areas, where we must use risk reduction measures to get back into the Low Danger zone. This seems like a simple, obvious concept, yet most avalanche accidents occur because we choose terrain too dangerous for the snowpack conditions.

terrain. And the only time you can go to dangerous terrain is when you have a safe snowpack. It's as simple as that.

The risk equation works on all scales. First I start with the big picture (pretrip planning), then move to the intermediate (mountain) scale, and finally look at the critical local (slope) scale (Figure 9-3). Below is an example of how I revisit and tweak this risk equation throughout the day.

Pretrip Planning

The avalanche advisory helps us answer the three most important questions:

❖ What kind of avalanche are we dealing with?

❖ What's the pattern?

❖ How will the forecasted weather affect the stability?

Let's take the advisory in Figure 9-4. Persistent slabs are the main problem of the day. The locator rose and the discussion tell us that this is a typical faceted snow weak layer, which exists mostly on mid and upper elevation shady aspects (northwest-, north-, northeast- and east-facing slopes). The heat of the sun has either prevented the faceted layer from forming on the south- through west-facing slopes or has destroyed it after it formed. The weak layer has been buried by a couple of storms, so we have a relatively stiff slab overlying the weak layer—like a pane of glass on top of a pile of potato chips.

This kind of avalanche is your basic nightmare—difficult to trigger, but if you do, very large and dangerous—which is why this type of setup accounts for so many fatalities. In other words, it's low probability and high consequence. It's that

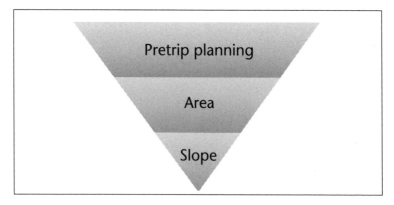

Figure 9-3. A relationship diagram of the three levels of avalanche information gathering depending on geographic scale.

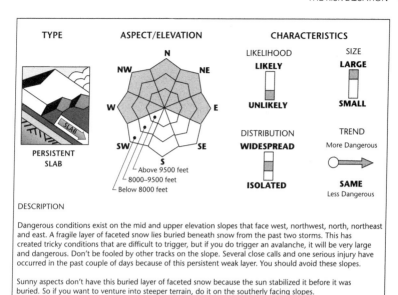

TYPE

PERSISTENT SLAB

ASPECT/ELEVATION

Above 9500 feet
8000–9500 feet
Below 8000 feet

CHARACTERISTICS

LIKELIHOOD — LIKELY / UNLIKELY

SIZE — LARGE / SMALL

DISTRIBUTION — WIDESPREAD / ISOLATED

TREND — More Dangerous / SAME Less Dangerous

DESCRIPTION

Dangerous conditions exist on the mid and upper elevation slopes that face west, northwest, north, northeast and east. A fragile layer of faceted snow lies buried beneath snow from the past two storms. This has created tricky conditions that are difficult to trigger, but if you do trigger an avalanche, it will be very large and dangerous. Don't be fooled by other tracks on the slope. Several close calls and one serious injury have occurred in the past couple of days because of this persistent weak layer. You should avoid these slopes.

Sunny aspects don't have this buried layer of faceted snow because the sun stabilized it before it was buried. So if you want to venture into steeper terrain, do it on the southerly facing slopes.

Figure 9-4. A typical avalanche problem from an advisory

Russian roulette scenario but this time there's one 44 magnum bullet loaded into a pistol that has 50 chambers. This is a Dirty Harry situation; how lucky do you feel?

I wouldn't have a very long career (or life) if I regularly pulled the tail on that kind of beast. So for me, the choice is easy—I always avoid slopes with monsters lurking in the basement unless I can keep my slope steepness under about 25 or 30 degrees and not locally connected to anything steeper. So now, looking at the advisory, I know the pattern. I can safely recreate on the sunny aspects (south through west) but I absolutely have to avoid avalanche terrain on the shady aspects (north through east). No exceptions (this is my Ulysses Contract for the day).

The secondary avalanche problem (shown in a secondary advisory, see Figure 4-1) is wind slabs along the upper elevation ridges. Strong winds from the north deposited these wind slabs, which means that we will find them mostly on the wind-exposed, southerly facing slopes. But since wind swirls around a lot in the mountains, we could find wind slabs on almost any slope. Luckily, wind slabs are easy to recognize and avoid because they are right on the surface and we can spot them by their characteristic smooth, rounded shape. So now we know to keep our avalanche eyeballs peeled to look for wind slabs, and we simply avoid them.

That means that our destination for the day will be low and mid elevation south- and west-facing slopes without any obvious wind slabs. If the riding conditions are horrible on those aspects and we absolutely HAVE to be on the shady aspects, we can probably recreate safely on 25 to 30 degree slopes that are not locally connected to steeper ones.

The next step: I form a mental picture of the terrain available to me today. If I'm headed to an unfamiliar area, I pull out the maps or consult Google Earth to get a feel for the lay of the land. Since the snowpack conditions don't allow me to travel with abandon, I need to be very careful to choose terrain that allows for a lot of route choices. I don't want to get boxed in by choosing what the Canadians call "complex" terrain—multiple, overlapping avalanche paths with few choices to avoid avalanche terrain (see Chapter 2). Today is the day I need "simple" terrain—mostly low angled, or heavily treed, terrain with many route choices, and any steeper terrain must be south or west facing.

This is where someone who reflexively goes to their familiar slopes where they always find good powder will often get into trouble. The avalanche report tells me specifically to avoid exactly those slopes (shady slopes where I usually find good powder). Persistent weak layers have to be matched with equally persistent patience. I often head to south-facing slopes during or right after storms because that's the only time they will have good powder. The sun will quickly crust them up so this is my only chance to enjoy them. This way I give another few days for the persistent weak layers on the shady slopes to stabilize. Alas, such is life—so many seductive temptations that are best avoided until the timing is right. Patience, my friend, patience.

Next, I look at the weather forecast to see how the weather will affect the instability. Will the weather make it better or worse? Will the weather control our destination? Poor visibility means we need to stick to the trees to avoid whiteout conditions on open slopes. Wind means we need to avoid upper elevation, wind-exposed terrain. Strong sun and melting conditions mean we need to avoid southerly facing slopes. Heavy or deep snow from a recent storm means that we need to be on a steep slope to get going (on skis or a board), so we have to choose a slope with a stable snowpack (often going to a resort is the best option on deep days). Deep days mean I may get the snowmobile stuck so perhaps groomed trails are the best option. Rain means I should head to high elevation terrain where the precipitation is snow instead of rain. Sunny, clear weather means I have the visibility to get into the upper elevation, alpine terrain. And so on.

Finally, I can choose my partners for the day. Since dangerous conditions exist, I need partners who are knowledgeable, skilled, and disciplined. Today is not the day for a large, unskilled, and unsupervised group. Someone who does not know about the critical importance of aspect would quickly get into trouble if they suddenly bolted off onto the wrong slope.

Intermediate (Mountain) Scale

As we drive to the general destination, we continue to look for obvious clues (five red flags) and continue to discuss our options. Notice I almost always like to keep my options open until the last minute. I make my mountain decisions by continually updating my beliefs and plan based on the latest evidence. Known as the "Bayesian" approach, this works well for most things in life, especially for critical mountain decisions that could kill us. I almost always avoid having specific destinations or goals. Pay attention. Look ahead. Be nimble and quick.

When I look at the terrain with my avalanche eyeballs, Figure 9-5 is how I see it. I see forbidden terrain, "maybe" terrain, and safe terrain. Seeing with avalanche eyeballs is my x-ray vision. Thus, armed with some knowledge, avalanche skills, and the proper equipment, I am in almost total control of my destiny.

Figure 9-5. The shaded areas represent forbidden terrain because the buried layer of faceted snow exists on the east- and north-facing slopes we can see here. The south-facing slopes (facing the left side of the photo) do not have any buried layers of faceted snow, making them much safer. The gentler slopes on the lower right foreground would be a good combination of safer terrain and safer snowpack.

At the trailhead, I always do a beacon check with everyone in the party—no exceptions. We do a last-minute equipment check and talk about the general plan for the day—the general destination, where we should stop and regroup, what time we need to be back, and known hazards to watch for. Before leaving cell phone coverage, I always text our intended destination to someone who will miss me if I don't return that night. Others do the same.

Local (Slope) Scale

Once we start traveling on the snow everything gets easier, at least for me. Suddenly, I'm not thinking academically about the avalanche problem, but instead I can use my senses to feel it, smell it, hear it, see it, and breathe it in. This is where my lifetime spent in the snow pays off because 10,000 unnamed sensations and millions of long-forgotten memories marinate in my unconscious mind. Intuition.

Yet the analysis process must continue. I keep checking for red flags. Every 100 yards, I poke my pole into the snow or dig down with my hand to check the layers and bonding. I regularly step off the trail into undisturbed snow to see how it feels and responds. I jump on small test slopes—the road bank, the side of a stump, or

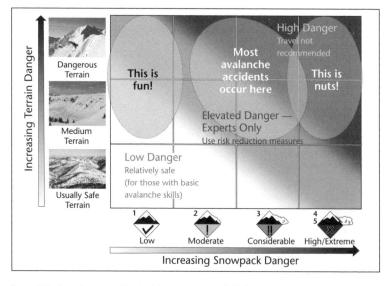

Figure 9-6a. Low danger combined with dangerous terrain is fun. Dangerous snowpack combined with dangerous terrain is nuts. Most avalanche accidents occur because people choose terrain that is more dangerous than the snowpack will allow. It's all too easy to push it too far.

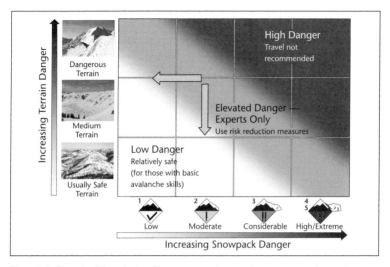

Figure 9-6b. To get back into the Low Danger zone we have to choose safer terrain or safer snow-pack.

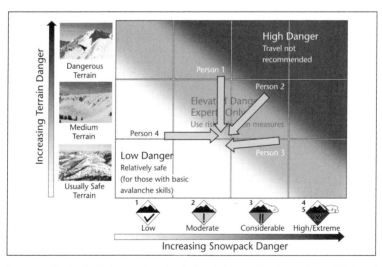

Figure 9-6c. The key to staying alive in avalanche terrain is to continually update your beliefs and plans throughout the day with each new piece of evidence. Each group member often has different beliefs and plans, but by continuously gathering information and continually updating beliefs and plans based on that information, the group will usually converge on the same combination between snowpack hazard and appropriate terrain.

Figure 9-7. Based on our step-by-step decision-making process, this is the safest route, both ascending and descending, based on steepness, consequences, and the direction the slope faces (southeast). If we travel on skis or a snowboard, our ascent route needs to be extra safe since we travel much slower, people tend to be grouped closer together, and we have limited escape routes because we have climbing skins attached to our skis or are on snowshoes. On the descent, we can sometimes choose more hazardous terrain because we can travel one at a time and keep our speed up; we thus have more escape-route options. For snowmobilers, the ascent and descent routes tend to be more similar. The terrain in this bowl has medium consequences for triggering an avalanche, meaning that we have at least some options to survive being wrong about our snow stability assessment. (Remember, we can only enter high consequence terrain when we have extremely stable snow.)

other small slopes. I notice where other parties are traveling and carefully watch to see how the snow responds when they tweak the steeper slopes. I cut cornices to send them down the slope ahead of me (first making sure no one is below).

I also like to get out my shovel and dig at least one (preferably several) quick snow profiles to test the deeper weak layers. Snow profiles provide me with extremely valuable information but they require a lot of training and experience to interpret, which is beyond the scope of this book.

Mentally, I'm constantly weighing the danger of the snowpack against the danger of the terrain (See Figure 9-2 and Figure 9-6a). If I'm not in the Low Danger zone, I adjust my route to choose safer terrain or safer snowpack (Figure 9-6b).

Often at the beginning of a tour, everyone in the group has a different opinion on where we are on the snowpack-terrain diagram, but as we gather more information throughout the day, usually the group will settle into a consensus around the correct combination (Figure 9-6c). If the group disagrees, it means that you need to (1) gather more information, (2) do a better job of communicating, or (3) someone is wrong.

Our final route and terrain choice might look something like Figure 9-7.

I also do a final review of all the various biases and mental shortcuts that affect all of us, and I try to identify any problems with human factors. How might we be wrong? What would the newspaper headline say tomorrow if we were? Is there anyone in our group who is not feeling it? Are there any dissenting opinions?

If I have properly paid attention and done my homework, by the time I arrive at the slope that could kill me or one of my friends, I already have almost all the information I need to make the final, critical choice—whether I decide to bet with my life.

Now, for the final exam. We commit to the slope and find out whether we were right or wrong. As we know, unforeseen events may occur and we may make mistakes. Therefore, we always need to think big and prepare for the worst. We use all of our low risk travel rituals:

- ❖ Go one at a time.
- ❖ Have an escape route preplanned.
- ❖ Never go first.
- ❖ Never trust a cornice.
- ❖ Be obsessed with consequences.
- ❖ Start small and work your way up.
- ❖ Communicate.
- ❖ Use a belay rope when appropriate.
- ❖ Use the right equipment.
- ❖ Remember: terrain, terrain, terrain.

Figure 9-8 is a simple overview of the whole process. These are the step-by-step components of avalanche safety, starting with the large geographic scale and ending on the specific slope. Once we decide to commit our life to a specific slope or route, we practice low-risk travel to further minimize the danger. Figure 9-9, the Avalanche Smart Card, is a simple checklist I like to use to remind me of all the critical pieces of information I need to check and in what order. When we decide whether we commit to a slope that could kill us, we have to balance the danger of the snowpack with the danger of the terrain; see Figure 9-1. We may combine a dangerous snowpack only with safe terrain, and the only time we can go to dangerous terrain is when we have a safe snowpack. The person in the picture reminds

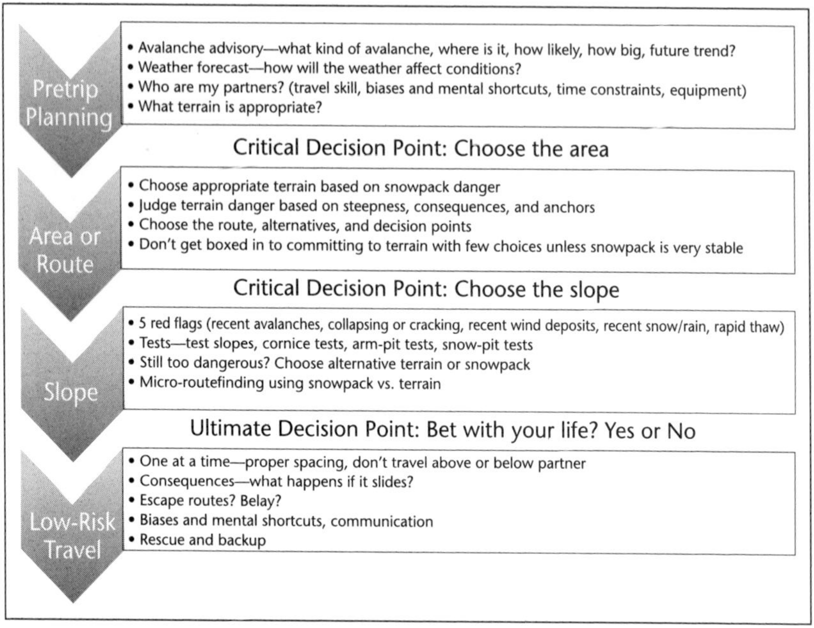

Pretrip Planning	• Avalanche advisory—what kind of avalanche, where is it, how likely, how big, future trend? • Weather forecast—how will the weather affect conditions? • Who are my partners? (travel skill, biases and mental shortcuts, time constraints, equipment) • What terrain is appropriate?

Critical Decision Point: Choose the area

Area or Route	• Choose appropriate terrain based on snowpack danger • Judge terrain danger based on steepness, consequences, and anchors • Choose the route, alternatives, and decision points • Don't get boxed in to committing to terrain with few choices unless snowpack is very stable

Critical Decision Point: Choose the slope

Slope	• 5 red flags (recent avalanches, collapsing or cracking, recent wind deposits, recent snow/rain, rapid thaw) • Tests—test slopes, cornice tests, arm-pit tests, snow-pit tests • Still too dangerous? Choose alternative terrain or snowpack • Micro-routefinding using snowpack vs. terrain

Ultimate Decision Point: Bet with your life? Yes or No

Low-Risk Travel	• One at a time—proper spacing, don't travel above or below partner • Consequences—what happens if it slides? • Escape routes? Belay? • Biases and mental shortcuts, communication • Rescue and backup

Figure 9-8. Step-by-step decision making process

us that various human factors always bias our perceptions and beliefs about the evidence in front of us. Our biases always place a "thumb on the scale" of the critical balance between the danger of the snowpack and the danger of the terrain. If we decide to commit our life to the slope, we proceed to the next step of low-risk travel where we deal with the exposure and vulnerability parts of the risk equation.

Various countries around the world (Canada, Switzerland, France, and Austria) have developed several "decision aids" in which the user adds up numbers based on various observations and evidence to yield a numeric answer about your relative risk. These decision aids have been somewhat controversial because the complexity of the avalanche phenomenon does not lend itself to simple algorithms. Yes, these decision aids help for most common avalanche situations, but they can never cover all the subtleties we can encounter or unusual conditions. This is why I prefer to stick with simple conceptual diagrams and checklists, like those I have presented in this book: They simply remind us to consider what we have learned from field-based avalanche classes, books and videos. I don't discourage people

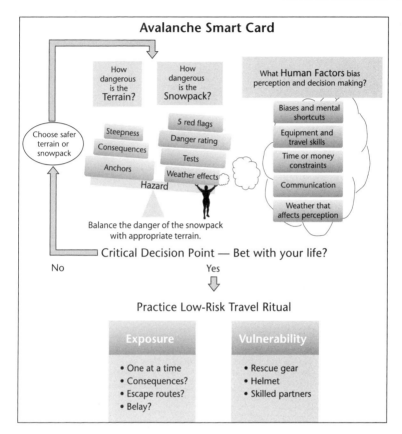

Figure 9-9. Here is my simple checklist to use for slope-scale decision making, an Avalanche Smart Card.

from using numerical decision aids, but remember that nothing can replace a reputable, multiday, field-based avalanche class, plus a lot of personal experience.

FINAL TAKE-HOME POINTS

Just because you have read this book does not mean you are an avalanche expert. This book on avalanche essentials is more like a learner's permit. We learn about avalanches not by reading or watching a video or lecture; we learn about

Photo 9-2. These big fractures from a large, deep-slab avalanche occurred on a very gentle 20-degree slope, which is possible only if it's locally connected to steeper terrain. Below this photo, the terrain rolls over into a very short section where the slope is 32 degrees. Even though some friends of mine triggered this slope from gentle terrain, when the collapse propagated into terrain steep enough to slide, it pulled much of the gentler slope snow along for the ride. One person, standing on gentle terrain, was pushed into a tree and buried 6 feet deep. He survived only because his partners executed a textbook-perfect rescue and got him breathing barely in time. Take-home point: Especially in very unstable conditions, gentle slopes are only as safe as the terrain they are locally connected to.

avalanches by doing. With the information in this book, you now need to get into the mountains and start practicing until it all becomes intuitive. But that takes time, usually several years of practice. Here are some techniques for practicing your avalanche skills:

❖ Most important: Go out on the high-danger days and find a small test slope (3–6 meters high / 10–20 feet) where you can trigger avalanches in a safe environment. Wallow around in unstable snow, feel it, taste it, thump it, cut it up, jump on it—and it will teach you everything you need to know.

❖ Avoid overconfident people. Recognize avalanche experts by their humbleness and conservative decisions. Follow them and learn from them.

- ❖ Thirty-degree slopes can be a lot of fun. Save extreme terrain for extremely stable snow conditions.
- ❖ Remember that most of what we believe is not true, so make only evidence-based decisions.
- ❖ And, finally, unforseen events will occur and we all make mistakes. So always be prepared for the downside.

RESOURCES

AVALANCHE PUBLICATIONS

American Avalanche Association. *The Avalanche Review*. www.americanavalancheassociation.org. A must-have magazine for avalanche professionals.

Avalanche Canada. www.avalanche.ca. Nonprofit organization that issues daily avalanche forecasts throughout winter for much of the mountainous regions of western Canada.

Canadian Avalanche Association. *The Avalanche Journal*. www.avalancheassociation.ca. Periodical publication that is a must-have magazine of important avalanche information and research in Canada.

Fredston, Jill, and Doug Fesler. *Snow Sense: A Guide to Evaluating Snow Avalanche Hazard*. 5th ed. Edited by Karl Birkeland and Doug Chabot. Anchorage: Alaska Mountain Safety Center, 2011. This is the most popular avalanche book ever written and is highly recommended, especially for beginning avalanche students.

Haegeli, Pascal. *Avaluator 2.0*. Canadian Avalanche Center. www.avalanche.ca/cac/store/books.

International Snow Science Workshop Proceedings. http://arc.lib.montana.edu/snow-science/. This international conference occurs in North America on even-numbered years and, recently, in Europe on odd numbered years. This conference is the leading vehicle for publication of both scientific and practitioner avalanche literature. Its motto, "Merging of Theory and Practice," says it all. The proceedings are not peer reviewed, but rather constitute a vehicle for scientists and practitioners to freely publish and exchange ideas. Montana State University has generously posted the proceedings from all ISSW conferences on their website.

Jamieson, Bruce. *Backcountry Avalanche Awareness*. Revelstoke, BC: Canadian Avalanche Association, 2000.

Jamieson, Bruce, Darcy Svederus, and Lorie Zacaruk. *Sledding in Avalanche Terrain: Reducing the Risk*. Revelstoke, BC: Canadian Avalanche Association, 1998.

Jamieson, Bruce, and Jennie McDonald. *Free Riding in Avalanche Terrain: A Snowboarder's Handbook*. Revelstoke, BC: Canadian Avalanche Association, 1999.

Jamieson, Bruce, Pascal Haegeli, and Dave Gauthier. *Avalanche Accidents in Canada*. Revelstoke, BC: Canadian Avalanche Association, 2010. A compilation of avalanche accidents and statistics for 1996–2007.

LaChapelle, Edward R. *Field Guide to Snow Crystals*. Cambridge, UK: International Glaciological Society, 2001.

LaChapelle, Edward R. *Secrets of the Snow: Visual Clues to Avalanches and Ski Conditions*. Seattle: University of Washington Press, 2001.

Logan, Nick, and Dale Atkins. *The Snowy Torrents: Avalanche Accidents in the United States 1980–86*. Special Publication 39. Denver: Colorado Geological Survey, 1996.

McClung, David, and Peter Schaerer. *The Avalanche Handbook*. 3rd ed. Seattle: Mountaineers Books, 2006.

Münter, Werner. *3x3 Avalanche Assessment Process & Reduction Method*. Brooks Range Mountaineering Equipment Co, 2007. http://m.cdn.blog.hu/fo/foka/file/3x3 _assessment.pdf. Summary in English of Werner Münter's method, *3x3 Lawinen*, which was published in German.

Snow, Weather, and Avalanches: Observation Guidelines for Avalanche Programs in the United States. 3rd Edition. Victor, Idaho: American Avalanche Association, 2016.

Tremper, Bruce. *Staying Alive in Avalanche Terrain*. 2nd ed. Seattle: Mountaineers Books, 2008.

Williams, Knox, and Spencer Logan. *The Snowy Torrents: Avalanche Accidents in the United States, 1996–2004*. Victor, Idaho: American Avalanche Association, 2017.

WEATHER BOOKS

Whiteman, C. David. *Mountain Meteorology: Fundamentals and Applications*. New York: Oxford University Press, 2000.

Williams, Jack, and *USA Today*. *The Weather Book: An Easy-to-Understand Guide to the USA's Weather*. 2nd ed. New York: Vintage Books, 1997.

Woodmencey, Jim. *Reading Weather: Where Will You Be When the Storm Hits?* Helena: Falcon-Guides, 1998.

FIRST-AID BOOKS

Auerbach, Paul S. *Medicine for the Outdoors: The Essential Guide to Emergency Medical Procedures and First Aid*. 4th ed. New York: Lyons Press, 2003.

Isaac, Jeffery. *The Outward Bound Wilderness First-Aid Handbook*. New York: Lyons Press, 1998.

Schimelpfenig, Todd, and Linda Lindsey. *NOLS Wilderness First Aid*. 3rd ed. Mechanicsburg, PA: Stackpole Books, 2000.

Weiss, Eric. *Wilderness & Travel Medicine: A Comprehensive Guide*. Seattle: Mountaineers Books, 2011.

Wilkerson, James A., ed. *Medicine for Mountaineering & Other Wilderness Activities*. 6th ed. Seattle: Mountaineers Books, 2010.

GENERAL MOUNTAINEERING BOOKS

Eng, Ronald C., ed. *Mountaineering: The Freedom of the Hills*. 8th ed. Seattle: Mountaineers Books, 2010.

Volken, Martin, Scott Schell, and Margaret Wheeler. *Backcountry Skiing: Skills for Ski Touring and Ski Mountaineering*. Seattle: Mountaineers Books, 2007.

BOOKS ON HUMAN FACTORS AND DECISION MAKING

Kahneman, Daniel. *Thinking, Fast and Slow*. New York: Farrar, Straus, and Giroux, 2011.

Shermer, Michael. *The Believing Brain: From Ghosts and God to Politics and Conspiracies—How We Construct Beliefs and Reinforce Them as Truths*. New York: Henry Holt, 2011.

Silver, Nate. *The Signal and the Noise: Why So Many Predictions Fail—But Some Don't*. New York: Penguin, 2012.

Taleb, Nassim Nicholas. *The Black Swan: The Impact of the Highly Improbable*. 2nd ed. New York: Random House, 2012

Tetlock, Philip, and Dan Gardner. *Superforecasting: The Art and Science of Predicting*. New York City: Broadway Books, 2015.

AVALANCHE VIDEOS AND DVDS

Canadian Avalanche Center. www.avalanche.ca/cac/training/resources/videos. Canadian Avalanche Center has a great compendium of published avalanche education videos available online. You can also entertain yourself for endless hours by watching all the video clips on YouTube. In addition, each of the major avalanche centers regularly publish video tutorials and video field observations; find these at Avalanche.org by clicking on the local avalanche center.

The Fine Line: A 16mm Avalanche Education Film. DVD. Sherpas Cinema, 2008. Professionally produced and very high-quality avalanche instruction video featuring most of the top avalanche education professionals in Canada.

Know Before You Go. YouTube. Utah Avalanche Center, 2012. http://www.youtube.com/watch?v=hE3RUrjB7Mc. This exciting and entertaining 17-minute avalanche primer is most people's first stop on their avalanche education journey. You can view it for free on YouTube.

Time is Life: Medical Training in Avalanche Rescue. DVD. CISA-IKAR, Newport Studios, 2006. http://www.time-is-life.org/. Available in ten languages, this video illustrates protocols for avalanche rescue recommended for advanced users and avalanche and medical professionals.

White Risk. Swiss Institute for Snow and Avalanche Research. CD. http://whiterisk.org/. A slick, interactive CD available in English and available for download purchase online.

WEBSITES

American Avalanche Association, www.avalanche.org. Official website of the American Avalanche Association. Supported and run by avalanche professionals, it offers one-stop shopping for a wealth of avalanche information and links to a multitude of other avalanche sites. It also provides links to local avalanche centers, which list local classes, and lists national avalanche education providers.

Canadian Avalanche Association, www.avalancheassociation.ca. One-stop shopping for avalanche information in Canada.

European avalanche centers, www.slf.ch/laworg/map.html.

International Association of Snowmobile Administrators, www.snowmobilers.org/saferider/homepage/page_00.html. Avalanche education for snowmobilers.

Swiss Institute for Snow and Avalanche Research, www.slf.ch/welcome-en.html.

INDEX

Boldface page numbers refer to tables or figures. *Italicized page numbers refer to photographs.*

ABOUT THE AUTHOR

Bruce Tremper grew up skiing in the mountains of western Montana and learned about mountains and avalanches from his father at a young age as well as from avalanche professionals. He was trained in the "avalanche system" since the late 1970s doing avalanche control at Bridger Bowl Ski Area and studied with some of the top avalanche scientists in the country while earning a master's in geology at Montana State University. He has also worked doing mountain rescues in both Grand Teton

National Park and Glacier National Park, served as director of avalanche control at Big Sky Ski Area in Montana, and worked with avalanche forecasters Jill Fredston and Doug Fesler at the Alaska Avalanche Center. For nearly three decades, he has served as director of the Utah Avalanche Center and was in charge of backcountry avalanche preparations for the 2002 Winter Olympics in Salt Lake City. He has been featured in dozens of national and international television documentaries and news programs on avalanches, including ones produced by National Geographic, the Discovery Channel, PBS, and the BBC. He is the author of the best-selling *Staying Alive in Avalanche Terrain*.

MOUNTAINEERS BOOKS

SKIPSTONE   BRAIDED RIVER

recreation · lifestyle · conservation

Mountaineers Books is a leading publisher of mountaineering literature and guides—including our flagship title, *Mountaineering: The Freedom of the Hills*—as well as adventure narratives, natural history, and general outdoor recreation. Through our two imprints, Skipstone and Braided River, we also publish titles on sustainability and conservation. We are committed to supporting the environmental and educational goals of our organization by providing expert information on human-powered adventure, sustainable practices at home and on the trail, and preservation of wilderness.

The Mountaineers, founded in 1906, is a 501(c)(3) nonprofit outdoor activity and conservation organization whose mission is "to explore, study, preserve, and enjoy the natural beauty of the outdoors." One of the largest such organizations in the United States, it sponsors classes and year-round outdoor activities throughout the Pacific Northwest, including climbing, hiking, backcountry skiing, snowshoeing, bicycling, camping, paddling, and more. The Mountaineers also supports its mission through its publishing division, Mountaineers Books, and promotes environmental education and citizen engagement. For more information, visit The Mountaineers Program Center, 7700 Sand Point Way NE, Seattle, WA 98115-3996; phone 206-521-6001; www.mountaineers.org; or email info@mountaineers.org.

Our publications are made possible through the generosity of donors and through sales of more than 800 titles on outdoor recreation, sustainable lifestyle, and conservation. To donate, purchase books, or learn more, visit us online:

MOUNTAINEERS BOOKS

1001 SW Klickitat Way, Suite 201 • Seattle, WA 98134
800-553-4453 • mbooks@mountaineersbooks.org
www.mountaineersbooks.org

OTHER MOUNTAINEERS BOOKS YOU MIGHT ENJOY

Staying Alive in Avalanche Terrain, 2nd edition
Tremper
Accessible and engaging guide to keeping
safe in avalanche country

**Avalanche Pocket Guide:
A Field Reference**
Tremper
Waterproof quick reference for evaluating
and managing avalanche danger

**Backcountry Skiing: Skills for Ski
Touring and Ski Mountaineering**
Volken, Schell, and Wheeler
Essential instruction for backcountry skiers

**Snow Travel: Skills for Climbing,
Hiking, and Crossing Over Snow**
Zawaski
Learn to manage year-round
snow travel—and go where
you want, anytime you want.

**Mountain Travel & Rescue:
National Ski Patrol's Manual for
Mountain Rescue**, 2nd edition
National Ski Patrol
The official rescue workbook of the National
Ski Patrol teaches mountain travel, survival,
search and rescue, and more.

Don't Freeze Out There! Deck
Winter outdoor survival tips in
a fun and functional full deck

**Mountaineers Books has more than
800 outdoor recreation titles in print.**
For more details, visit
www.mountaineersbooks.org